HERE IS CHELSEA

HERE IS CHELSEA

Reflections from The Chelsea Society

Edited by Jane Dorrell

With a foreword by Tom Pocock

Elliott & Thompson

London

CONTENTS

CONTENTS

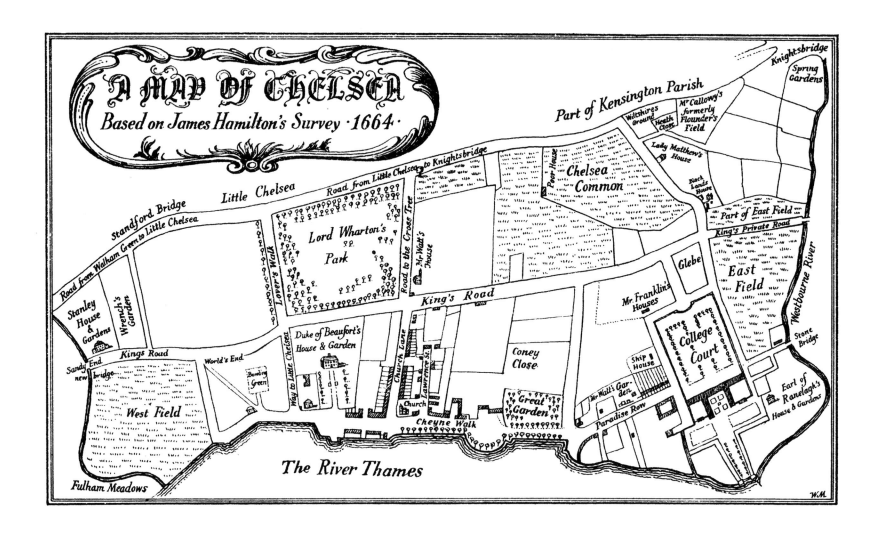

'By what means the time is so well-abbreviated I know not,
except weeks be shorter in Chelsey, than in other places!'

Extract from a letter of Queen Katharine Parr
to the Lord High Admiral Seymour, written from Chelsea, 1547

FOREWORD

Tom Pocock

Only the rich and the old can live in Chelsea nowadays, it is sometimes said. There is some truth in this when cottages built for Victorian artisans sell for more than £1,000,000. Even so, there is something about the square mile of the Royal Borough of Kensington and Chelsea to the immediate north of the Thames that defies the image presented by smart magazines and the cult of the celebrity. Partly this is due to the scale and fabric of the place: the balance between width of street and height of houses; the number of trees and gardens; and always the great river sliding past.

But it is more than that. There is an inherited character, which may not be as strong as it once was but which survives. This comes partly from what Chelsea was before the mid-l9th. century: both fashionable outer suburb and small industrial town, its industries being those generated by fashion – porcelain in particular – and by transport, notably the transhipment of cargoes from river to road. Then, with the building of stucco-fronted Belgravia and the covering of the Fulham market-gardens with streets of little red-brick houses, Chelsea was absorbed in London yet kept an originality by becoming the artists' quarter of the capital.

Chelsea has long been a transient place. Not so long ago it would be said that everybody had lived in Oakley Street when it was a street of lodging-houses. Even those of us who can remember the Old Church before it was bombed and rebuilt, the sailing barges on the river, the Chelsea Palace music-hall and the candle-lit Blue Cockatoo restaurant in Cheyne Walk, were once newcomers themselves, or our parents were.

Times and fashions swing, particularly in Chelsea, it seems, and not only in the King's Road. As the great houses of Mayfair became offices so the grand residential district moved west. When the well-to-do migrants arrived in Chelsea, the impact was easily absorbed. This had long been a balanced community, where rich, poor and those in the middle lived, mixed up together, within one square mile in a social harmony that town planners strive and fail to reproduce. In recent years there have been just more of the well-to-do; some would say, rather too many for a healthy balance.

Yet the character remains. Sadly, it is seldom to be found in the local shops and pubs, so many of which are gone, or are going. But it still survives here and there: in the few remaining artists' studios, in Chelsea's churches, in the amiable raffishness of the Chelsea Arts Club – and in the Chelsea Society. This consists of more than a thousand individuals and individuality is essential to the character of Chelsea.

The Society was founded in 1927 to foster the amenities of Chelsea by which must be meant that character. The great battles the Society has fought with authority – sometimes winning, sometimes losing – have usually have been about planning issues. They have fought for the preservation of beautiful and historic buildings, the limitation of the height and scale of new development, the control of traffic and much else. Yet it is upon such practicalities that character depends as much as upon personal characteristics.

These, too, the Society helps to keep alive through its other activities: meetings, outings, lectures and publications, of which this book is an example. The Society is, through its general and specialist committees, involved in the present and future. This book shows that it is also aware of the past that made Chelsea what it still is. It shows what could be achieved when, or if, the Society secures Council support for a Chelsea Museum to enshrine that past, such a focal point of education and entertainment as flourishes in Hampstead, Richmond and Wandsworth.

So here is a collection of articles that have appeared in the annual Chelsea Society Report, introducing some of the people and places involved. What a collection! Lily Langtry and Whistler, Thomas Carlyle and Bram Stoker, Queen Elizabeth 1 and Walter Greaves, Sir Charles Dilke and Thomas Crapper, Leigh Hunt and Sir Thomas More, Sir Hans Sloane, of course, and many more. We visit the houseboats on Whistler's Reach, the Royal Hospital, Ranelagh and Cremorne, the legendary Pheasantry and the Chelsea Bun House. Those who have regularly read the Report and attended the Society's lectures will know that this is only a piquant taste of the Chelsea banquet.

Savour this and a walk through Chelsea will acquire a fresh, inimitable quality.

QUEEN ELIZABETH I AS A GIRL IN CHELSEA

Elizabeth Longford

Kensington Palace unquestionably stands in a "Royal Borough". But the ghost of Henry VIII's vanished Manor House gives a passing substance to the idea of "Royal Chelsea". Princess Elizabeth, Henry's daughter by Anne Boleyn, lived in Chelsea Manor House during a dangerous and turbulent period of her adolescence. It may have influenced her and, through her, English history more than people today imagine. "Royal Chelsea" may have a historical, if no longer visible, meaning.

The history of Henry's Manor House is quickly told. The King acquired the manorial rights of Chelsea from Lord Sandys in 1536. He then built on the banks of the Thames where now runs Cheyne Walk, a typical Tudor manor, castellated and quadrangular with cellars, halls, parlours and kitchens, drawing-rooms, bedchambers, closets and a gallery. The gallery will feature prominently in our story. Today all that remains of Chelsea's Tudor palace are some russet bricks in the garden walls of Cheyne Walk between Oakley Street and Chelsea Manor Street; and, beyond the end wall of Cheyne Mews, some mulberry trees which were possibly planted by Queen Elizabeth I. However, as a girl living in Chelsea Manor House, Princess Elizabeth was to do many more exciting things than plant mulberries.

There is no better beginning to the story of Elizabeth and Chelsea than the words of John Bowack, Chelsea's earliest historian, written a hundred years after Elizabeth's death.

They have an excited ring:

'Twas here the renowned Princess Elizabeth (afterwards Queen) was Nurst (which would) for ever render this Place Famous, and make its name out-last Time.

The "nursing" of Princess Elizabeth was not altogether an easy task, especially in regard to her teeth. Her governess Lady Bryan wrote:

God knoweth my lady hath great pain with her great teeth and they

come very slowly forth, which causeth me to suffer her Grace to have her will more than I would. I trust to God an 'her teeth were well graft, to have her Grace after another fashion than she is yet, so as I trust the King's Grace shall have great comfort from her Grace.

But Henry VIII was at present bent on getting "comfort" from his subsequent wives rather than his daughter, having executed Elizabeth's mother, Anne Boleyn. Indeed he neglected Elizabeth so shamefully as a child that she had "neither gown, nor kirtle, nor petticoat, nor no manner of linen." As for her teeth, we hear of them causing Queen Elizabeth I much agony in old age also. Possibly her noted abstemiousness over food was due in part to permanent toothache. By the time she was six her father had grown into a mountain of fat. She may also have picked at her food in order not to become like him.

Meanwhile her early education was faring much better than her teeth. At six she could read English well and began Latin, besides being proficient with her needle. Her religious life was in full swing next year, so that it is not surprising to find her composing her own miniature Book of Devotions thirty years later. What is surprising about this tiny volume (the copy in the British Library is 3 x 2 inches) is the tone of melancholy. For instance, this extract from one of the two English prayers in the book:

Thou seest whereof l came of corrupt seed: what l am, a most frail substance: where I live in the world full of wickedness: where delights be snares, where dangers be imminent, where sin reigneth, and death abideth. This is my state. Now where is my comfort? In the depth of my misery I know no help but the height of thy mercy...

Her troubled childhood may have made its contribution to this typical prayer.

Elizabeth could dimly remember her mother; her second stepmother, Jane Seymour (her first, Anne of Cleves, had been quickly put aside by Henry) died after the birth of Elizabeth's half-brother Prince Edward. To be sure, things began to look up when the attractive young Catherine Howard, Elizabeth's first cousin once removed, became Henry's fifth wife; we hear of Elizabeth receiving two small presents of jewellery from her while at Chelsea. But eighteen months later it was discovered that Catherine Howard had been no "Virgin Queen" on marriage, and had had lovers afterwards. Like Elizabeth's own mother, Catherine lost her head in a bloody public execution at the Tower. The little princess, her cousin, was only eight. But she told Robin Dudley, a boy companion of her own age, that she would never marry.

No doubt marriage in general was becoming synonymous in the child's mind with death. But it was her father's sixth wife, Catherine Parr, who was to brief the adolescent Elizabeth in the intensely personal horrors of marital unhappiness – not with Henry VIII, who died in January 1547, but with Thomas Seymour, who married Henry's widow while aspiring to be Elizabeth's husband.

Henry's marriage to Catherine Parr had taken place in 1543. Parr was the bride's maiden name, her brother being Earl of Northampton. In fact she was already an immensely rich widow with the added attractions of chestnut hair, a tall athletic figure, a good intellect, a merry wit and ardent nature. To Henry she seemed just what he needed. To her, Henry was a sacred vocation. She deemed it her duty to marry him once he proposed marriage. In her own words, Henry's sixth wife would be a good woman at last – "none adulterer, nor fornicator, and so forth." (Though what more heinous crimes the 'so forth' stood for is obscure!)

Nevertheless Catherine was passionately in love with another man and he with her. The other man was Thomas Seymour, uncle of the future Edward VI, but for the present still only a country gentleman.

For some three or four years, the young Prince Edward and Princess Elizabeth seemed to have a mother again in Catherine Parr. Elizabeth gave her a beautifully embroidered book made by herself as a New Year's present for 1545. Besides being a mark of affection for her stepmother it was also a testimony to the progress the Princess was making in her education, thanks partly to Catherine's interest. Hitherto Elizabeth had been taught by her lady-in-waiting, Mistress Catherine Ashley, a well-educated and much-loved friend whom she called Kat. But now she was allowed to share her half-brother's tutors; first the Rev. Richard Cox and then the great Cambridge scholar; John Cheke.

Elizabeth's love of learning was such that Cheke soon recommended a tutor for the Princess' sole use, Grindal, another Cambridge scholar but still in his twenties. The Princess's tutors were all serious, devout Protestants. No card-playing, no dancing for this child, though later on by the time she was sixteen this had changed and the Princess was to learn "in the Italian manner to dance high". She would always enjoy dancing, whether high or low. At Chelsea her gayest moments were probably spent outdoors, for

she liked to be as much as possible in the open air. The qualities of Chelsea air were famous and the waters of the Thames were sweet and flowed softly. Elizabeth's schoolroom curriculum would have been Greek and the New Testament in the mornings and Cicero or Livy in the afternoons, with French and Italian fitted in somehow.

Suddenly there was a hiccup in this excellent "royal progress". Her father died when she was in her fourteenth year. Her half-brother became the boy-king Edward VI. And the Seymour family took over the government, albeit without a firm grip, Thomas Seymour's elder brother Edward becoming the Lord Protector Somerset, while Thomas landed the powerful prize of Lord High Admiral and the title of Baron Seymour of Sudeley.

Thomas's ambitions were higher than the Admiralty. The obvious next step was to acquire a valuable wife. Even during Henry's life-time he had set his cap at more than one great heiress but he was still a lusty bachelor in 1547 and not out of his thirties. Handsome, with brilliant small eyes and a bushy beard, he had a way with women. His language was as full of oaths as it was of jokes, both of them imbued with characteristic Tudor coarseness. He would lard his dialogue with blasphemous references to "God's precious soul" and once sent a messenger to Kat Ashley with the request to know 'whether her great buttocks were grown any less or no?' Soon Seymour would be able to see for himself, for he was to live in the same house as Kat Ashley and her young mistress, the Lady Elizabeth, for many pregnant months.

After Henry's death, Seymour stepped up his quest for a wife with an audacity that created many rumours but also a certain amount of mystery. It was said that he considered Mary Tudor and then half-sister Elizabeth, but could not get permission to marry either from the Council. Then he tried Anne of Cleves, again with-out success; and finally returned to the courtship of his old, well-endowed love, Queen Catherine Parr. Two potential queens and two ex- or former queens – not bad going at all.

Catherine's passionate temperament responded with ardour to their first clandestine meetings; clandestine, because it was essential for them to get married before telling the Council they had done so. They would thus face the Council with a *fait accompli*.

In the early spring dawns Seymour would glide through the wicket gate to the north of Chelsea Manor, having silently crossed the fields that surrounded the house. He would find the Queen waiting for him in her bedchamber. In another bedroom the Princess Elizabeth and Kat Ashley were quietly sleeping, with the Princess's personal maids not far off. There was also the tutor, William Grindal, somewhere in the house, and her cofferer Thomas Parry, as well as a retinue of servants. But no one was the wiser when some time in April – the date is still uncertain – the Lord High Admiral secretly married Queen Catherine Parr and came to live with her in Chelsea Manor House.

The presence of this boisterous incarnation of masculinity under a hitherto chaste roof could hardly fail to influence the young Princess. She was at a sensitive stage of adolescence. Her most recent biographer, the American historian Carolly Erickson has drawn a beguiling portrait of the Princess at this age, in her *The First Elizabeth* (1983):

She was growing tall, and acquiring the watchful self awareness of a young woman, part vanity, part defensiveness. A portrait painted some time in early adolescence catches a hint of steely vigilance in her grave, unsmiling stare – or perhaps she was merely trying to look regal. We who know what her future was to hold can read much into that tight-lipped countenance: self control, resolute modesty, even defiance. The forced maturity in the expression is touching, for the face has not quite lost its childish contour. Still, what is telling about the portrait is how the intelligent power of Elizabeth's expression overwhelms all else – the elegance of her crimson kirtle and embroidered gown, her restrained adornments of pearls and yet, her sloe eyes, bright red hair and milk-white skin, clear and free of the pimply 'wheals' that 'disgraced the faces' of sixteenth-century adolescents, even her remarkable hands, their long spider-thin fingers holding a velvet-bound book.

Elizabeth would need all the "vigilance" and "defensiveness" of which she was capable. For Seymour was no sooner established in Chelsea as a married man than he began visiting her in her bedroom before she was properly dressed. His early morning greeting would be a jovial slap "upon the back or on the buttocks". Kat Ashley, who slept in the same room, would shout, "Go away for shame", while Elizabeth blushed with a mixture of embarrassment and excitement. Her household soon noticed that she coloured and smiled at any mention of his name. Kat's role seems to have been ambiguous. Though apparently shocked by Seymour's behaviour, she was careful to tell Elizabeth that Seymour had wanted to marry *her – for herself.*

Elizabeth at first defended herself against Seymour by getting up earlier and earlier. But Seymour was not to be defeated. One day he burst in with his wife in tow and together they tickled Elizabeth in bed until she screamed with hysterical laughter. Another time he besieged the Princess and her dressers behind the bedcurtains, calling to her, "Come out." The scandal grew; particularly as the Lord High Admiral had taken to barging in wearing no uniform but a dressing-gown – "barelegged in his slippers".

It was in the gallery that Kat Ashley at last tried seriously to put a stop to a deteriorating situation. She met Seymour by appointment in the gallery and told him that his brazen conduct was damaging the Princess's fair name: her own chastity was being called in question. The big man's reply was bluster and a volley of "God's-precious-soul".

Meanwhile his wife Catherine was pregnant. Possibly her judgment was affected by the difficult time she was going through physically, for she tried to protect Seymour by telling Kat that Elizabeth was being seduced not by Seymour but by *another man.* Seymour, she said, had "looked in at the gallery window, and saw my lady Elizabeth cast her arms about a man's neck." Elizabeth denied the story and Kat believed her. In fact there were no suitable candidates for a seductive scene in Chelsea Manor House but Seymour himself. The Princess's tutors were all too high-minded; especially Roger Ascham, who had by now taken Grindal's place. The famous Ascham had come from Cambridge to Chelsea like Grindal before him. Though Ascham's appearance was cheerful he tolerated not the slightest interruption to his pupil's studies. It was her excellent mind that he admired, and through him she was to emerge from the Seymour cauldron into the clear light of learning.

As Catherine's time drew near, the suspect pair – her husband and step-daughter, grew more reckless. At last the crisis broke. Catherine found Elizabeth and Seymour alone one day, Elizabeth in his arms. The Princess's period of residence at Chelsea came to an abrupt termination. She left for the shelter of Sir Anthony Dening's home in Cheshunt, where she remained in poor health throughout the summer. The unfortunate Catherine's health, however, was a thousand times worse. Her miserable pregnancy ended in the birth of a girl and the death of the mother, perhaps from puerperal fever. She expired on 5th September 1548, denouncing her unfaithful husband in a frenzy of grief. Two days later Elizabeth reached the age of fifteen.

After Catherine's death the fever seemed to transfer itself to her husband. He was believed to be plotting to seize power after committing three murders – of the delicate young king, his brother the

Protector and Princess Mary – and marrying Elizabeth. He was caught shooting a guard-dog in the King's palace, sent to the Tower and executed.

The backwash of scandal and terror for a time besmirched Princess Elizabeth, particularly as her lady Kat Ashley and her cofferer Thomas Parry were also sent to the Tower, for questioning. Slanderous tongues asserted that Princess Elizabeth was the "Little Whore" just as her mother Anne Boleyn had been the 'Great Whore'. It was said that she too was in the Tower, pregnant by the Lord High Admiral. A midwife could even be cited who had already delivered her of Seymour's child, which was then 'miserably destroyed'. Elizabeth replied to an inquisitorial storm with outraged denials and growing power and confidence. By the end of 1449 she was welcomed back to her half-brother's court with colourful splendour.

Princess Elizabeth, however, had been through the fire and a bright worldly image was no longer her choice, or indeed safe. She returned as a modest maiden preferring to wear simple black or white rather than elaborate fashions and a dazzle of jewels. No longer would she bridle and blush at the mention of any man's name. She was deeply religious, almost a "born-again" Protestant, but with the self-knowledge born of suffering.

Many years later she was to compose a sad love poem celebrating a recently broken romance, of which the following was the first verse:

When I was fair and young and favour graced me,
Of many was I sought their mistress for to be,
But I did scorn them all and answered them therefore,
Go, go, go, seek some other where,
Importune me no more.

Today Elizabeth's harrowing experiences between the ages of thirteen and fifteen would be considered quite enough to prevent her ever afterwards from making a happy marriage. Added to that was the fact that in her child's memory, marriage more than once meant the block. The Tower and Chelsea between them were enough to redirect the royal line through the descendants of James I; and to preserve Elizabeth in celibacy and safety as the Virgin Queen.

1983

Reprinted with the kind permission of Lady Antonia Fraser

The
Annual General Meeting
of the
Chelsea Society
will be held at
THE TOWN HALL, CHELSEA
on
Wednesday, February 20th, 1946

———

Tea 5 p.m.   Meeting 5.45 p.m.
followed by an Address by
WALTER H. GODFREY, Esq.
F.S.A., F.R.I.B.A.
on

"CHELSEA OLD CHURCH, ITS PAST AND ITS FUTURE"

———

Visitors will be welcome.

R.S.V.P. to
Mrs. Cockburn, J.P.,
2, Cheyne Gardens,
S.W.3.

MORE IN CHELSEA

Marie Ney

Thomas More's estate in Chelsea at the time of his judicial murder was a large area of land extending northward from the river at Lindsey House to where Kensington Gardens now are. It contained farms, cottages and almshouses, as well as his own mansion set in 34 acres of park and gardens.

Professor Scarisbrick, in a lecture delivered during a More Quincentennial Conference in Bronx, NY, stated that: 'As the King's Officers set about gathering the dead man's possessions they came across the fact that on 25 March 1534, just before More had to face the oath and when he would have known the end was at hand, he conveyed some of his possessions – in Chelsea and Middlesex – to a trust... The discovery brought a swift response – an act of parliament declaring the conveyance null and void and referred to his "corrupt and malicious mynde ...after his said treasons resorted to this stratagem".' Much was lost in this dissipation of the contents of the Great House: the Library, the treasures collected by More not for their value but for their fine workmanship, and, important to us, documents, letters, leases, etc., which might tell us why Thomas More selected this area, Chelsea, to live, when he came, and when he bought the land. The dates given for the purchase range from 1520 to the generally accepted one of 1525.

Richard Hyde, one of More's medical protégé's and tutor at times to the School, dates an introduction to Margaret Roper's English translation of Erasmus on the Paternoster 'at Chelsey the year of our Lord 1523 the first day of October'. There is also evidence that Thomas More and his family lived in a smaller house when first in Chelsea – a house, later 'The Farm' where Lindsey House now stands.

The harmony of the Great House in Chelsea must have been largely due to the character and housewifery of Alice More, who has received less than her due from writers on More. She has been called illiterate, and in a preface to one of Yale University editions of a More work, she is described by the editor as 'a strong-willed, ignorant woman'. Strong-willed possibly, but ignorant? Would

Thomas, when Jane died, have married an ignorant woman to care for their four small children (of whom Margaret was aged 6 and the youngest, John, just over 2)?

Thomas More would have known Alice. Her husband, John Middleton, who died in 1509, is described as 'citizen and mercer of London and merchant of the Staple (a sort of customs house) at Calais.' Thomas More had been 'Granted freedom of the Mercers Company' and he conducted 'negotiations on behalf of the Mercers with the Pensionary at Antwerp' in 1509.

Left a widower in the summer of 1511 and desperately needing a mother for his children, what could have been more sensible than his swift remarriage – the lady being willing – to someone whose deceased husband he must have known if only superficially? Older than More by some seven years this lady would have brought her knowledge of housewifery to the marriage, a jointure and a daughter who became as devoted to her stepfather as his own daughters.

Erasmus is said to have been unfriendly to Alice when he stayed at Bucklesbury during his last visit to England in 1517. R.W. Chambers describes him at this period as 'a man of importance: the dedication of his New Testament had been accepted by Leo X'. It must have been during that visit that Alice and Erasmus were unfriendly. She was different to the girl wife of earlier years. Erasmus had been younger, perhaps less demanding, and was enthralled by the translations he and More were making from the Greek satirist Lucian. With Erasmus, too, More was enjoying the writing of *Praise of Folly*, which was dedicated to More. They were also hopeful that by criticising the abuses of the church they could help to reform them. More was especially enjoying the success of his Lucian translations – a greater success in his own time than his *Utopia* would be later: Lucian had nine editions, *Utopia* six. But in 1517 Erasmus was travel-tired, perhaps becoming less hopeful of Church changes. At Bucklesbury there were five children, all of school age, there was the School, not only for the More children but for others as well. All this would not leave Alice much time to cosset a visitor whose Latin she couldn't understand and who had no English. But the dislike must have been superficial. Writing to Margaret Roper in 1529 Erasmus tells of his great joy 'when the painter Holbein unveiled for me the painting of your whole family done with such felicity... I have written this to you dear Margaret so please see your sisters know it is addressed to them no less than yourself... to that elegant Lady Alice your mother give my fond greeting and be sure to commend me to her lovingly. I was pleased

Sir Thomas More and family, after a Holbein painting

to kiss her portrait since I could not kiss her person'. Past dislike is here obviously forgotten, and there could even be the friendly special joke for Alice; she would have known how the English habit of kissing delighted Erasmus 'where-ever you go you are received with kisses: when you leave you are dismissed with kisses when you go back your kisses are returned to you'.

Hans Holbein's portrait delighted Erasmus in 1529 – a year in which, in September, the harvest of the More estate was burnt. Sir Thomas was at Court where he wrote to Alice: 'I am informed by my son Heron of the loss of our barns and our neighbours' also with all the corn therein'. He leaves it to his wife 'to advise somewhat with your friends what way were best to take for provision to be made for corn for our household and for seed this year coming'. It was a serious matter to lose a harvest for a big estate which would have so many depending on that harvest and on the seed too. The loss of the barns was no less serious, shortening days allowing fewer hours for the rebuilding.

But having put the problem in the hands of his efficient housewife, Thomas More adds that Alice must be of good cheer and 'take all the household with you to Church and there thank God for what he has given and for what he has taken... for his wisdom better seeth what is good for us than we do ourselves...' That Church was the Old Church in Chelsea, much rebuilt after our century's bombing but some of its fabric, especially in the More Chapel, the same where Alice walked with her household to make Christian acceptance of the lost harvest.

Erasmus gives us a vivid picture of the family home in Chelsea, though he was never there. It must have been from his many young protégés who were given hospitality by Lady More that he learned of the home and family, especially from the famous young painter, Hans Holbein, who lived in the house for two years. Writing to John Faber, Bishop of Vienna, in 1532 Erasmus says: 'More has built for himself on the banks of the Thames not far from London a country house dignified and adequate without being so magnificent as to excite envy – Here he lives happily with his family... There is not any man living so affectionate to his children and he loveth his old wife as if she were a girl of fifteen.' That Alice loved him spills over into her two halting letters on his behalf, one at Christmas 1534 to Henry pleading for her husband: '... his long time service diligently done to your Grace... his offence is not governed by... obstinate mind but of such a long... and deep-rooted scruple as passeth his power to put away.' And this in 1535 to Master Thomas Cromwell: '... the cause of my writing in my extreme necessity... I do pay weekly 15 shillings for board wages of my poor husband and his servant for the maintaining whereof I have been compelled to sell part of mine apparel... I humbly beseech your good mastership for the love of God... to show favourable help in comforting my poor husband and me in our great necessity.'

A small Exhibition dedicated to Blessed Thomas More was held in 1929 in Beaufort Street Convent. At it G. K. Chesterton, who was among the speakers, said that 'Thomas More was above all things historic: he represented at once a type, a turning point and an ultimate destiny. If there had not been this particular man at this particular moment the whole of history would have been different'.

1978

RANELAGH

'The Divinest Place under Heaven' Fanny Burney

Jane Dorrell

Oh that the designers of the ill-fated Millennium Dome had looked back to the middle of the eighteenth century and seen how it should have been done. For sixty-one years Ranelagh Gardens and its great amphitheatre drew enthusiastic crowds. Rather different from the snide comments of the press today, newspapers of the time described it as: 'A place of pleasure which is not to be equalled in Europe, and is the resort of people of the first quality'.

It was in the 1690s that Viscount Ranelagh, Paymaster General to the forces, built himself a mansion to the east of the Royal Hospital. Around it, on land granted to him by William III for an annual lease of £5, he laid out gardens which were: 'Curiously kept and elegantly designed'. They extended from the old burial ground in the north, to the river marshes in the south, and to what is now the Chelsea Bridge Road in the west. The great north-south avenue of the gardens is the central artery of today's Flower Show. At his death in 1712 the property was inherited by his daughter, then in 1733 it was sold by her trustees to James Lacy, a co-patentee with David Garrick of the Drury Lane Theatre. The idea was to turn it into a place of public entertainment – a pleasure garden after the manner of Vauxhall which lay across the river. But delays caused by the opposition of the authorities of the Royal Hospital and escalating costs – that sounds familiar – meant that it was not till 1741 that the necessary capital was raised by selling 36 shares of £1000 each and William Jones, the architect of the East India Company, was commissioned to design an amphitheatre in the grounds. It is hardly surprising that there was opposition to this grandiose scheme. Lord Ranelagh had also been Treasurer – and it could be added Embezzler – to the Royal Hospital from 1689 until 1702, when he was rumbled by suspicious auditors and expelled from the House of Lords. Suffice it to say that his chicanery caused the opening of the Hospital to be delayed by two-and-a-half years after

he squirrelled away some £70, 000 for his own use. In 1707 he was pleading poverty – signing his letters 'poor old Ranelagh'. But in the end the terms of the lease were unbreakable and, however galling it was to them, the commissioners were unable to hold out. Work on the rotunda started at the end of 1741 and curious sight-

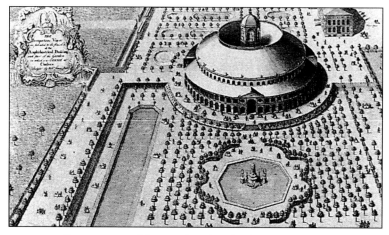

Perspective view of the rotunda and gardens by William Jones.

seers were able to watch the erection of: 'A noble structure, inferior to few publick buildings in Europe'. It was comparable in size to the Reading Room at the British Museum. At the same time, with theatrical productions in mind, the gardens were redesigned with arches and long vistas. Dr Johnson, thirty years later, said, 'The *coup d'oeil* is the finest thing I have ever seen'.

In the weeks prior to its official opening the public was admitted to a series of public breakfasts. The twenty-four-year-old Horace Walpole, that egregious follower of fashion, could not miss such a spectacle. He wrote to Horace Mann in Florence: 'I have been breakfasting this morning at Ranelagh Gardens. They have built an immense amphitheatre... and the building is not finished but they get great sums by people going to see it... there were yesterday no less than 380 persons, at 18 pence a-piece'. On May 24th 1742 he was at the official inauguration. 'Two nights ago the Ranelagh Gardens were opened at Chelsea; the Prince, Princess, Duke, much nobility and much mob besides, were there. There is a vast amphitheatre, finely gilt, painted, and illuminated, into which everybody that loves eating, drinking, staring, or crowding, is admitted for twelve pence. The building and disposition of the gar-

Canaletto's *The Avenue at Ranelagh*

dens cost sixteen thousand pounds. Twice a week there are to be ridottos, at guinea tickets, for which you are to have a supper and music. I was there last night, but didn't find the joy of it'.

The charge for admission was half a crown which included a *regale* of tea, coffee, bread and butter. It was open on Mondays, Wednesdays and Fridays during the season which began at Easter and ended in July when leaders of society disappeared to their country seats. By 1746 the orchestra stand had been moved from its original place in the centre to the side, where the acoustics were better, and a great stove replaced it in the centre. The heat this provided, regulated by an ingenious coating of tin plates which could be removed or augmented according to the weather, meant that occasional winter dances could be held.

The evening concerts were a draw from the beginning but the only other amusement – apart from breakfasts which were popular in the early days but which were soon banned as being a threat to public morals – was the endless parade round the vast interior of the rotunda admiring and being admired. This obviously suited

Walpole fine, but what was the attraction for those less fashion conscious? W.S. Lewis in his *Three Tours Round London* has a likely explanation for the success of Ranelagh for *hoi polloi* as well as gentry; the former could take their place in the galleries and watch everyone who was anyone parade endlessly before them. It was a first port of call for visitors from the Continent. A German, Carl Philipp Moritz, wrote in 1782: 'It is impossible to describe the effect it had on me when coming out of the gloom of the garden, I suddenly entered a round building, illuminated by many hundred lamps; the splendour and beauty of which surpassed everything of the kind I had ever seen before. Everything seemed here to be round; above there was a gallery, divided into boxes; and in one part of it an organ with a beautiful choir, from which issued both instrumental and vocal music. All around, under this gallery, are handsome painted boxes for those who wish to take refreshments; the floor was covered with mats; in the middle of which are four high black pillars; within which are neat fire-places for preparing tea, coffee and punch; and all around also there are placed tables, set out with all kinds of refreshments. Within these four pillars, in a kind of magic rotunda, all the beau monde of London moved perpetually round and round'.

Satirists had a field day, among them 'Harlequin' who wrote in the *London Magazine*; 'Fashion, dear bewitching Fashion, is my nocturnal pursuit. I paid my half-crown and walked into Ranelagh... upon my word, I thought no circular motion could affect my whirligigg head; but before I had been there half-an-hour, I had the vertigo strong. I know nothing but a mill horse that is still bound to go in one circle, unless it is the asses that turn round the mill in Ranelagh...' The 'asses' read like a roll call of familiar eighteenth century names. It was patronised by royalty, the aristocracy, politicians and most of the contemporary literati whose letters and novels have left us with vivid pictures of what it must have been like at Ranelagh during its heyday. Among the frequenters was Lord Chesterfield, of whom Lady Townsend wrote: 'Lord Chesterfield is grown so excessively fond of Ranelagh that he goes there every night and declares that he designs to live there soon altogether'. Smollett, who lived close by, wrote about it in *Humphrey Clinker*, and Evelina, Fanny Burney's eponymous heroine spends many 'gay and thoughtless' evenings there. Dr Johnson visited it often – though it is hard to imagine him joining the parade. In 1772 he said; 'when I first entered Ranelagh it gave an expansive and gay sensation to my mind such as I never experienced anywhere else'.

The only time the promenaders were interrupted in their eternal circling was at 7 o'clock when the sound of a bell gave notice that a particular performance was about to begin. Among the many popular singers and instrumentalists of the day one or two names stand out. Dr Burney – Fanny's father – became the regular organist, Handel wrote music for the fireworks which were to become a feature towards the end of the century and the eight-year-old Mozart amazed the throng when he played the harpsichord one night in 1764 accompanied by his father and sister. This event was trumpeted in the Public Advertiser. 'The celebrated and astonishing Master Mozart, lately arrived, a child of seven years of age (sic) will perform five Pieces of his own Composition on the Harpsichord and the Organ, which has already given the highest Pleasure, Delight

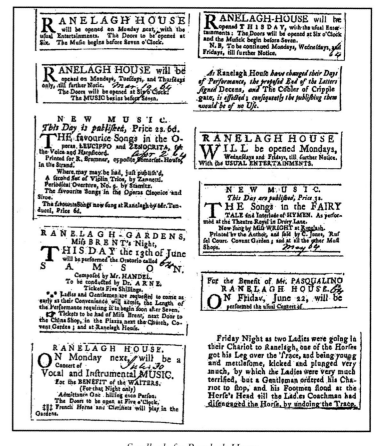

Small ads for Ranelagh House

and Surprise to the greatest Judges of Music in England and Italy.'

Richard Owen Cambridge, another contemporary satirist, surmised that the concept of Ranelagh was inspired by Henry VIII who introduced masquerades to England and to show them off 'caused to be built a banqueting-house 800 feet in compass like a theatre'. A great gale tore off the roof of Henry's 'dome' the very night it was completed, but no such disaster befell the rotunda at Ranelagh and in 1749 the first masquerade took place. It was held to celebrate the peace of Aix-la-Chapelle and it must have been a magic night. Who better to tell us about it than Walpole. 'It was by far the prettiest spectacle I ever saw; nothing in a fairy tale ever surpassed it. It began about three o'clock and, about five, people of fashion began to go. When you entered you found the whole garden filled with masks and spread with tents, which remained all night very commodely. In one quarter was a Maypole dressed with garlands, and people dancing round it to a tabor and pipe and rustic music, all masked, as were all the various bands of music that were disposed in different parts of the garden; some like huntsmen with French horns, some like peasants, and a troop of harlequins and scaramouchers in the little open temple on the mount. On the canal was a sort of gondola, adorned with flags and streamers, and filled with music, rowing about. All round the outside of the amphitheatre were shops, filled with Dresden china, japan &c, and all the shop-keepers in mask. The amphitheatre was illuminated; and in the middle was a circular bower, composed of all kinds of firs in tubs from twenty to thirty feet high. Under them orange-trees with small lamps in each orange, and below them all sorts of the finest auriculas in pots; and festoons of natural flowers hanging from tree to tree… There were booths for tea and wine, gaming tables and dancing, and about two thousand persons. In short, it pleased me more than anything I ever saw.'

Mrs Elizabeth Montagu, too, was at this masquerade. The 'Queen of the Bluestockings' was rather more scathing in her comments. She describes the costumes of the fashionable women present – among them Miss Chudleigh (later the Duchess of Kingston). Her dress sounds as though it might have been designed by Versace for a film première today: 'Miss Chudleigh's dress or rather undress was remarkable. She was Iphigenia for the sacrifice, but so naked, the High Priest might easily inspect the entrails of the victim… the Maids of Honour, not of maids the strictest, were so offended they would not speak to her'. It wasn't entirely a happy occasion. Mrs Montagu goes on to say that she: 'staid till 5 o'clock in the morning

and was not tired, but a glass of champagne and water gave me a fit of the colick the next day, and I have never been well since, but I had better luck than Miss Conway, who was killed by a draught of Lemonade she drank there…'

Ranelagh passed through a rough patch in the 1750s. In January and February 1750 earth tremors were felt in London. Influenced by John Wesley's proclamations that masquerades and such follies would bring down the wrath of God, Society fled the capital for fear of a third quake, which, although it didn't materialise, put a dampener on the season. In 1755 the earthquake in Lisbon gave some another pause for thought – but not for long. As Cambridge said: 'Great numbers of quality and people of fashion and distinction of both sexes, disguised themselves in all sorts of odd, antic and whimsical dress to prevent them being known, they all wore masques, and promiscuously rambled about in the rotunda and gardens, everyone being ready to mingle with the company without any distinction of sex, age or condition'. Fearful of the effect of these festivities on public morals the proprietors were refused a music licence for a year. If it had not been granted again the future would have been in doubt for, in the end it was to the quality of the music that the managers provided that Ranelagh owed its long life. And in fact, compared with Vauxhall, Ranelagh was remarkably free from rowdyism. It never became the haunt of prostitutes as Vauxhall did in its later years and Dr Johnson went so far as to describe it as a place of 'innocent recreation'. Samuel Rogers in his *Table Talk* describes it as being: 'so orderly and still, that you could hear the *whishing* sound of the ladies' trains as the immense assembly walked round and round'. The extreme fashions of the 1770s must have been another amusement for the spectators. Rogers adds: 'I have come to Ranelagh with a lady who was obliged to sit upon a stool placed in the bottom of the coach, the height of her headdress not allowing her to occupy the regular seat'. Everyone wore their best clothes to Ranelagh. No 'cropped heads, trousers or stockings' would have been admitted.

On one occasion though, there was trouble when four footmen were arrested for 'insulting several gentlemen by hissing those who didn't give or suffer their servants to take vails'. One was sent to Newgate and the other three were ordered to make public apologies. Perhaps the most memorable occasion in Ranelagh's long history was the regatta and ball which took place on June 23, 1775. The whole river was covered with pleasure boats and the barges belonging to the City Companies of Brewers, Goldsmiths, Skinners,

Canaletto's *Interior view of the Rotunda at Ranelagh*

Stationers and Vintners. At 7.30 in the evening a cannon signalled the start and the procession moved from Westminster Bridge to Ranelagh where there was dancing and supper. Walpole, no longer a young man about town, moaned in a letter to Lady Ossory that: 'There were such crowds in the street that I could scarce pass home... and I think I will go no more to sights'. Indeed for the ultra-fashionable, a visit to Ranelagh had become something of an endurance test. There were highwaymen to contend with at Hyde Park Corner, and as Walpole wrote to Mann in 1777, 'The present folly is late hours. Everybody tries to be particular by being there too late; and as everybody tries it, nobody is so. It is the fashion to go to Ranelagh two hours after it is over. You may not believe this but it is literal. The music ends at ten; the company goes at twelve.'

The strain must have told on others, because its popularity suffered a decline until the 1790s when, under the auspices of Henry Angelo, firework displays were introduced, together with such attractions as the transvestite Chevalier D'Eon showing off his fencing skills, the Prince of Wales and the Duke of York strolling with their mistresses, Mrs Fitzherbert and Mrs Jordan; there were some

successful ascents in balloons which drew the crowds, and on one occasion there was a 'Venetian spectacle'. Angelo writes: 'In the garden there was a large sheet of water, on which were a number of boats full of men, armed with long poles. The boats were then divided into two parties, an equal number of men in each, and the amusement consisted of endeavouring to push one another into the water. The victory was won by those who succeeded in ducking most of their opponents. The dresses of the men were so gaudy, and covered with ribbons that with their finery, their sousings created the more merriment to the spectators'. But in spite of these jollities the end was in sight. By the turn of the century Ranelagh was no longer the attraction it had once been and the money men were at the gates. It opened for the last time on July 8, 1803 and was demolished two years later. There was a Chekhovian lament in *Knight's* London: 'Having made bankrupts of its latest proprietors, it is now about, most probably, to give place to the formidable array of bricklayers and carpenters, who already look upon its beautiful groves as their own, and can neither listen to the melodies of the birds nor to the glorious harmonies of the mightier human performers, for the ringing blows of the axe and the crash of the falling trees, which they hear as it were by anticipation'.

But as we know, the builders did not move in. In 1826 the Gardens were bought by the Royal Hospital and today visitors to the Flower Show flock to a different entertainment. Perhaps the best time to visit Ranelagh now is late on a summer evening when it is just possible to shut out the rumble of traffic on the Embankment, and instead, in the mind's ear, catch the distant strains of Mozart's harpsichord.

2000

Select bibliography

Angelo, Henry. *Reminiscences*. 1828; *Bluestocking Letters*. Selected by R Brimley Johnson. John Lane, The Bodley Head, 1926; Chancellor, E Beresford. *The Pleasure Haunts of London during four Centuries*. Constable, 1925; Boswell, James. *The Life of Johnson*, Ed Birkbeck Hill, OUP, 1934; Collections relating to Ranelagh in the British Library; *The Gentleman's Magazine*; Moritz, Carl Phillip. *Travels of Carl Philipp Moritz in England in 1782*. Pub 1926; *The Letters of Horace Walpole*, Ed Mrs Paget Toynbee, Clarendon Press, Oxford, 1903-1918; Wroth, Warwick. *The London Pleasure Gardens of the 18th Century*, Macmillan, 1896.

I JOHN FRANCIS, Servant to Lady Delves, in Albemarle-street, do with the greatest Submission ask Pardon of the Publick for the Insult I offered last Friday Night at Ranelagh; and do return my most grateful Thanks to those Gentlemen who have treated me with so much Lenity, and given me an Opportunity of warning my Fellow-Servants. JOHN FRANCIS his Mark, I.

WHEREAS I WILLIAM BRANDON, Servant to Mr. Belliard, was, on Friday Evening last, unfortunately milled by other Servants attending at Ranelagh Gardens, to insult several Gentlemen as they came out, by hissing those who did not give or suffer their Servants to take Vails, which occasioned great Confusion; and being apprehended in the Fact by a worthy Gentleman of whom I take this public Occasion to ask Pardon, and do sincerely promise never to offend in the like Manner, and hope it will be a Warning to all other Servants, whose Happiness like mine, must depend on their good Characters. May 4. 64

WHEREAS I RICHARD PHILIPPS d.d, with great Insolence, declare on Friday Night last at Ranelagh, that Lady Delves's Servant was unjustly taken into Custody by a Scoundrel of a Gentleman: and whereas in consequence of this, I was the next Day discharged by Col. Hodges: I do now make this publick Acknowledgment of my Offence, and intreat by this Method Forgiveness from those Gentlemen who were highly insulted by that Declaration. Witness my Hand RICHARD PHILIPPS.

The public apologies of the three footmen.

FLUSHED WITH PRIDE:
THE STORY OF THOMAS CRAPPER

Book review by *Noel Blakiston*

By Wallace Reyburn. Macdonald Unit 75, London (1969) 15/-. This interesting and amusing little book pays a worthy tribute to an unsung Chelsea hero. When so many lords and commoners have given their names to personal or domestic amenities – chesterfield, davenport, cardigan, wellington, macintosh, bowler, bloomer, gladstone, hoover, stetson – how is it that "crapper" has not (so felicitously) become a household word? The story of Thomas Crapper's life and work is here told, from his walking at the age of eleven in 1848 from Yorkshire to London, where he got a job with a master plumber in Robert Street, Chelsea, to his performance as the Royal Plumber at Sandringham and the provider of a royal blue velvet seat for Lily Langtry. The chapter headings include *Pull and Let go is Born, By Royal Appointment, Inventor at Work, Seating Accommodation.* There are many illustrations, showing Thomas Crapper, his works in Chelsea, mechanistic diagrams, Lily Langtry and some lovely decorated pans.

Pedestal Lion Closet, 1896

The Sultan with decoration, 1896

The disappearance of Crapper's at No.120, King's Road in 1966 is a date in Chelsea's history, and citizens of Chelsea, who keep this entertaining book in a certain place, will flush with pride.

1970

A BUN TO REMEMBER

Chelsea's Contribution to Gastronomy

Tom Pocock

Chelsea, like Yorkshire, Devonshire and Dundee, has achieved an agreeable form of immortality by inventing and giving its name to a food. Indeed the Chelsea bun has more of a mythology and iconography – and certainly more mystery – than any English confection that comes to mind. But this native of Chelsea was, for many years, mystified by the extraordinary appeal of a bun over three centuries.

Our bun, as most of us probably know it and certainly as we buy it in most chain bakeries, is a strip of dough dotted with a few currants which has been curled like a snail and lightly sugared on the top. Certainly this is nothing to excite such vast mobs as once jostled to buy it on public holidays at the confectioners' shrine, the Chelsea Bunn House.

The currant bun (if you will forgive me) seems unlikely to bear much resemblance to its early eighteenth century original "zephyr in paste", or the "great cakes frothed with sugar and decorated with streamers of tinsel", which Dean Swift described in his *Journal to Stella* in 1712. It must, I suppose, have been the equivalent of Walls' ice cream, Mars bars, and every other mass-produced sweetmeat, in the days when the principal delicacy at the nearby Ranelagh pleasure gardens was bread and butter. Certainly, like many great inventions, its recipe coincided exactly with an urgent, but perhaps unidentified, demand of public taste.

Probably the first buns were sold from booths on the Five Fields, between Chelsea and Westminster, where fairs were held on public holidays and which became the site of popular taverns and tea gardens. Swift recorded: "boys and wenches buzzing about the cake-shops like fairs, " and there were vendors, like the later muffin-men, crying "r-r-r-r-rare Chelsea buns!"

It was the Hand family which perpetuated the skill of creating the buns. Their commercial success enabled them to build an elaborate bun-house just to the east of Chelsea, opposite the entrance to Ranelagh in Wilderness Row, which is now Bloomfield Place. This has vanished totally, together with its competitors, but just across Pimlico Road from its site a contemporary establishment survives. There, as is inscribed in eighteenth century lettering on a date-stone, is Strombolo House, once a tavern and tea garden, now an antique shop.

The appearance of the Bunn House is recorded exactly in the Hands' trade-card engraved by Hogarth. It was a long single-storey building fronted with a colonnade and much decorated by the same sort of knick-knacks that filled Don Saltero's coffee house in Cheyne Walk. There were lead models four-feet high of Grenadiers presenting arms, a portrait of the Emperor of Persia and a model of the Bunn House itself with moving figures.

Four generations of the Hand family presided. One of them had been an officer in the Staffordshire militia and became a noted eccentric with a fondness for wearing a Turkish fez and a long dressing-gown. He was caricatured by Matthew Darly in 1773 as "Captain Bun Quixote attacking the Oven."

Darly also drew him as "The Bun Macaroni" in his series of London dandies, together with one of his extravagantly-dressed customers, "The Chelsea Macaroni" – the ancestor of our contemporary denizens of the King's Road.

The seal of approval was set upon the bakery by royal patronage. The second and third King George and their families gorged there, so setting a fashion which all London could emulate since the buns only cost one penny. The Hands also had their "commercials" in verse, doggerel and songs.

> *0 flour of the ovens! a zephyr in paste!*
> *Fragrant as honey, and sweeter in taste!*
>
> *As flaky and white, as if baked by the light,*
> *As the flesh of an infant, soft, doughy and slight.*
>
> *Prelates and princes, and lieges and kings,*
> *Hail for the bellman, who tinkles and sings,*
> *Bouche of the highest and lowliest ones...*
> *There's a charm in the sound, which nobody shuns,*
> *Of "smoking hot, piping hot, Chelsea buns!"*

King George III was so satisfied that he presented the Hands with five guineas in a silver tankard. The crowds were equally delighted and the bun was introduced into a pop song of the day:

As I was going to Chelsea one day,
I met with a pretty young girl on the way.
I kindly saluted, but this was her tone,
Why can't you be easy and leave me alone?

Let me alone and let me alone,
Why can't you be easy and let me alone?

I told her my name, it was harmless James,
I call'd her a thousand sweet delicate names.
I told her her heart was as cold as a stone.
No matter, says she, can't you let me alone?

I says, my dear love, I am not in my sun,
If you go to the Bun-house, I'll buy you a bun.
No, thank you, says she, I've got money of my own
To buy half a thousand, so leave me alone.

I says, my dear girl, with you I shall dine,
For at Finchback's I heard they sell very good wine,
And more than all that, there is wax-work to be shewn.
No matter, says she, can't you leave me alone.

I followed this damsel through field after field,
With a deal of persuasion, I brought her to yield.
Next day we were married, and she altered her tone,
And she teases me now if I let her alone.

The Bunn House continued well into the nineteenth century and a contemporary account records that "provided the weather was favourable, there were generally on Good Friday nearly 200,000 people collected in the immediate neighbourhood." On this day, in 1829, nearly a quarter of a million buns were said to have been sold but by that time there were other confectioners lining the road past the now derelict site of Ranelagh and time was short before Thomas Cubitt, the speculative builder, covered the Five Fields with his gleaming stucco terraces to create Belgravia.

In 1839, the Bunn House was sold and demolished and its knick-knacks auctioned for a few pounds. The lead grenadiers fetched £4 10s. and adorned a house in Eaton Place for a time before disappearing into the limbo of the antiques trade. As Cubitt went to

work, the *Penny Magazine* reported in 1844: "The Chelsea meadows are now covered with bricks, either making or drying or built up into houses… The far-famed Chelsea bun-houses have stepped back from the road where they formerly stood; they appear now as confectioners' shops in the line of houses forming the street…'

The buns continued to be baked in Chelsea and, for the Festival of Britain of 1951 a replica of the Bunn House was put up in Sloane Square. Recently, The Chelsea Bun, a coffee house and restaurant opened in the King's Road with plaster buns on its facade and dough buns inside.

But what *was* the Chelsea bun and how can its immortality be preserved?

Reginald Blunt, the historian of Chelsea, wrote in 1928 that its recipe was "something of a mystery" but that old Chelsea people had told him that it had been very rich, and full of butter, eggs, sugar, rind of lemon and spice but no fruit. Later, Blunt discovered a recipe published in an eighteenth-century cookery book and gave it to a Chelsea baker, who thereupon took it as his own copyright and that secret is lost.

Another recipe, said to have come from an old Chelsea family, was published in the *Chelsea News* twenty years ago. This runs: "Take 1lb. flour, 1/4 1b. lard, I oz. yeast, 3 oz. castor sugar, 2 eggs, 1/4 pint milk, 3 oz. currants, 1/4 teaspoonful salt, 1/4 teaspoonful of cassia (cinnamon). Cream the yeast and add the warmed milk. Rub lard into the flour and salt. Add the yeast, cassia, milk and eggs. Beat all well together with a wooden spoon. Put in a warm place to rise to double its size. Roll into a long strip and sprinkle on the currants and sugar. Roll up firmly and cut across in pieces about one inch thick. Place in a greased baking tin and pack well together with the cut side upwards. Stand in a warm place for about half an hour and brush over with egg. Bake for about 20 to 30 minutes." Doubling the currants and using brown instead of castor sugar might be an improvement.

Too many Chelsea buns that I have eaten have been dry, tasting of cotton wool. But there is one variety of Chelsea bun which is not only the one food to which I am now hopelessly addicted but which would, to me, explain the frenzy of greed that seems to have possessed eighteenth century bun-eaters. Alas, it is not to be had in Chelsea, but in Cambridge.

For half a century the most ambrosial Chelsea buns have been baked at Fitzbillies, the pastrycooks in Trumpington Street, near the Fitzwilliam Museum. Light, succulent and sticky, rich with butter and currants, they have filled generations of undergraduates and, for a quarter of a century, I have been unable to visit Cambridge without returning laden with buns to show Chelsea friends what the place has lost.

As I expected, the recipe is Top Secret but the proprietor has kindly given some guarded but valuable hints. Mrs. Annette Day writes: "We have been baking our Chelseas since 1920 from a recipe which has remained unaltered to this day. The particular flavour is obtained by using a special brand of brown sugar and cinnamon and, of course, nothing other than the very best Vostizza currants are used; finally, the buns are washed with syrup made from a very dark treacle."

It is to this that Chelsea has given its name. 0 zephyr in paste! What, one wonders, will future generations identify with Chelsea? 0 lost innocence!

1971

THE PHEASANTRY

A La Recherche du Faisan Perdu

———

Nesta Macdonald

The history of 'The Pheasantry', now exposed in the midst of desolation, has been the subject of much legend. However, legend wilts when faced with documentation, and the facts are far more fascinating.

Once upon a time there were pheasants at the bottom of that garden; the house was named when they moved in in 1865. Its modern life began when they left in 1878 and the Jouberts took it over in 1880; but the story had better begin by setting the scene.

Many people have the idea that 'The King's Road' was a highway and, in its Chelsea stretch, a busy village shopping street. Not so. The great palaces of Chelsea were built near the river. This was the highway; travel between the City and Whitehall and Chelsea was by boat. The busy east-west thoroughfare was Paradise Row (now forming part of Royal Hospital Road). The 'King's Road' was but a narrow track, and by 1719 had acquired such an evil reputation for footpads that George I wished to close it to the public between Sloane Square and Church Lane (Old Church Street). Yielding to local feeling expressed in a Petition which included Sir Hans Sloane himself amongst the signatories, the King granted local residents the right to use it. They were supplied with bronze tokens. It remained closed until 1830. This naturally retarded urban development.

Soon after 1800, the area west of Sloane Street began to change as the fields were commercialised. It became one ribbon-development 'garden centre'. Houses were needed for more workers, and the small streets adjacent to King's Road were built for this purpose.

Here is the story of the house which it is most convenient to call 'The Pheasantry' though it was about a hundred years old before it acquired this name. It has been put together from a study of maps, ratebooks, registers, and directories. Street numbering only started in 1859, when the numbers in King's Road were fixed as they still remain. 'Box Farm', built in 1686, and demolished in 1900, which occupied the site of the old Classic Cinema, was the clue in the early years.

Before examining the maps, look at the building itself. The evidence of the eye is especially clear on its Markham Street flank. There you can see two enlargements. The original house barely reached to the level of the balconies of the principal floor. As for the facade, I have pointed out for years that this was faced with Victorian, machine-made bricks, quite different from the older, handmade bricks of the main structure.

Miss Jane Smith, the Brick expert at the Science Museum, most kindly cast a practised eye over the wreckage. She pointed out the change in the size of the hand-made bricks used when there were enlargements, with the consequent change in the arrangement of the courses. Moreover, she observed that the old bricks were of poor quality (some half-baked), as was the bricklaying workmanship.

Early map-makers indicated the buildings in a sketchy and inconsistent manner. Sometimes they drew 'The Pheasantry' as a simple oblong, sometimes they gave it a stalk haphazardly placed either front or back. Sometimes they joined it in a straight line with Box Farm, sometimes – correctly – staggered slightly behind and west of it.

The first map, by Hamilton, was drawn in 1664, and printed, allegedly updated, in 1717. The 'updating' was incomplete, and left out Box Farm, a Jacobean building.

The second map, by John Rocque, shows Box Farm, with open space beside it.

It is on the third map, dated 1769, that the house we call 'The Pheasantry' is shown for the first time. This map exists only in one manuscript copy, owned by the Cadogan Estate.

After 1794, there were many maps, and alterations to the site can be easily followed. In 1836, Thompson drew in a long garden behind 'The Pheasantry', attractively laid out. A map of 1869-78 shows a trellised area, obviously the aviary, at the end of a shrunken garden.

Turning from the buildings to their occupants, the site is dominated by four families, each of which confusingly retained the same Christian name in many generations. The Samuel Bakers first arrived in 1763, left in 1774, and returned in 1864. Pullam Markham, the first of that surname, came in 1795, and died in 1804. The first John Evans appeared in 1790, starting a trail of Evanses which ended only in 1899, and who contracted at least one marriage with a Markham. In 1899, it was Pullam Markham Evans who put Box Farm up for sale. The tangle of these two families is

too involved to be worked out completely. The fourth family, the Jouberts, are a story in themselves.

In 1763, one Samuel Baker, purveying 'Greens and Milk' to The Vestry, paid rates of lOs. 6d. for a half-year on his first field.

In March 1766, a Mr. Will Hammond paid 6s. 8d. on 'House and Garden', which appeared for the first time. This was immediately taken over by Samuel Baker, who continued to add more fields to his list.

This first rating of the 'House and Garden' shows that it was built towards the end of 1765, and tallies with the maps and with the first brickwork. Incidentally, there is absolutely no connection whatsoever with the family of Earl Amherst, which never owned any land in the King's Road area.

Samuel Baker was obviously ambitious. Designated 'Merchant', he acquired addresses in Dockland by 1770, and in New Bond Street by 1774. He was also in Beaufort Street, Chelsea, which had practical advantages compared with the shut-off King's Road, as it was easy of access both by river and along Paradise Row.

Possibly the John Evans who sought election to The Vestry in 1826 was the son of the man who paid rates in 1790. The family ran the dairy farm, and organised the grazing on Chelsea Common. John Evans also had a shop at Sloane Square, where he was listed as 'Grocer and Tea Importer', and bought up many other properties round and about.

So far there is no indication as to Pullam Markham's vocation. The naming of Pullam Terrace and The Markhams is seemingly in tribute to his memory. It could be that on the occasion of a marriage in 1804, Pullam Markham bestowed Box Farm, or the money to buy it, upon an Evans, turning the family into freeholders, and earning this gratitude. The descendant, Pullam Markham Evans, was a Chartered Accountant, head of his own firm in Basinghall Street, when he sold Box Farm in 1899. His spinster sisters were living there until the sale, though he had removed to 25 Cheyne Walk, some years before.

One can see all these families as energetic, thriving, and moving up in the world.

There is a drawing on the sale catalogue, which shows Box Farm as three-storeyed, stuccoed, its facade typically early nineteenth-century, and its windows embellished with Coade Stone ornaments. These are identical with the model used on the west side of Smith Street, opposite, which was built about 1804. Whilst the interior had remained 'quaint', it looks as if the alterations modernising the

The Pheasantry, King's Road

exterior had been made then. Possibly 'The Pheasantry' was enlarged and even made to match at the same time. Its attic windows and roof correspond to many of that period in the district.

Aviaries were popular all over Europe, and trade in exotic birds was big business. Consul Swinhoe, "our man in Cathay", was only one servant of the Crown to add to his wealth by handling the export of live birds from China.

For many years, the directory entry of Samuel Baker was inconspicuous. In 1839 it suddenly appeared with this splendid spread, printed in beautiful large type:

> BAKER, Samuel C. and Charles N.
> Dealers in Ornamental Poultry, Live Wild Fowl, Gold, Silver, White,
> Pied and Common Tame-bred Pheasants and Poults, Foxes and Cubs for Stocking, etc. 3 Half-Moon Passage, Gracechurch Street.

Once the King's Road was re-opened to the public in 1830, it began to fill with all sorts of crafts and trades. No shortage then of painters, carpenters, or plumbers! One Mr. Edward Dench outgrew his premises in Box Cottage, nearer to Markham Square, and, in 1857, moved into 'The Pheasantry'. He paid rates for the dwelling and the workshops in which he made boilers for hot-houses. In 1860, a third count was added – Photographic Institute! But his tenure was not to last for long.

In 1864, the Samuel Baker of the day started paying the rates on 'House and Garden' once more, albeit curiously as a tenant.

And so, at long last – *Enter the Pheasants*.

The Bakers advertised from Beaufort street almost every week in *The Field*. The move was noted in their standard advertisement on 8th April, 1865:

> PHEASANTS. Messrs. Baker beg to invite their patrons, customers, and gentlemen interested in the breed of PHEASANTS to an INSPECTION at their new Establishment, 152 King's Road, Chelsea, of Specimens of the different varieties of the BREEDING-STOCK (Previous to being penned for the season), conspicuous amongst which will be the Versicolor or Japanese Pheasants, with first and second cross, which cannot fail to be interesting to all desirous of improving the breed.

Note the gentlemanly reticence – not a word is said about price!

However, a rival firm in Leadenhall Market advertised the same week: Philip Castang charged fifteen guineas for a pair of versicolor pheasants – no mean sum in 1865.

Pheasants were not the only creatures dealt in by the Bakers, though they seem to have dropped the foxes from their list. Another Baker advertisement had been running in *The Field* for a long time, classified under 'Farming'. On 18th April, 1865, it appeared with the address quietly altered:

> BRETONNE COWS. Original importers – gold medal was awarded to Messrs. BAKER, by the Royal Agricultural Society, for their Breton bull PRINCE, bred by themselves, and they beg to inform their customers of the arrival of another handsome HERD of these useful animals, calved and down-calving. Intending purchasers are respectfully invited to view the above, or to communicate for further particulars. Messrs. Baker have now completed their final arrangements for the importation of the above cattle (the same variety as originally imported by them) which, after many years' experience, regardless of expense and trouble, has enabled them to offer this pure breed of cattle at prices so low that only the sale of a large number will compensate the importers. The above must not be confused with the common cows of the country.
> The Pheasantry, 152 King's Road, Chelsea.

The reason for importing this particular breed is obscure. They were black-and-white cattle, and an expert said that "if fed plentifully, these will fatten readily, but bulls rapidly become so high-spirited that they are unmanageable". Add to this the fact that they are not heavy milkers, and it is even more mysterious.

But that is how, in April 1865, 'The Pheasantry' was christened.

From 1866 until 1878, the rates on House, Stables and Garden were paid by Charles Newcombe Baker, Bird Dealer, alone; he also had premises in Jubilee Place.

And so, in 1881 – *Enter the Jouberts*. Whence came this family whose name persists today in the flats they built in 1894 in Jubilee Place?

Here is their entry in the Post Office Directory for 1881:

> JOUBERT, Amédée and Son (late of 6 and 7 Percy Street, W.). Upholsterers, painters, gilders, ecclesiastical and domestic deco-

rators, cabinet makers, artistic furniture and parquet flooring manufacturers by patent machinery.
'The Pheasantry', 152 King's Road, Chelsea.

Though the family tree is incomplete, Jean-Baptiste Amédée Joubert was descended from a family of cabinet-makers of whom the most famous was Gilles Joubert, *ébéniste du roi* from 1763 until his death in 1775. His brother, Pierre, was a skilled *menuisier*. The family was strongly Royalist, and in later generations devoted to Louis XVIII and Charles X. (And, of course, they were not Huguenots.) Their arrival in Maddox Street in 1831 leads one to suppose that they followed Charles X into exile after the July Revolution of 1830. Four children were born there; William Amédée, the eldest, born 1831, died in Chelsea in 1907. Henry Charles Réné, born there in 1835, was baptised at St. George's, Hanover Square, in July 1836. He set up in business in Percy Street in 1867, and in 1869 married a Miss Francatelli, of Upper Chelsea, at Trinity Church, Sloane Street. Their only child, Felix, was born in Percy Street in 1872.

Maddox Street was in the heart of fashionable Mayfair; Percy Street in the district of skilled craftsmen. The move to Chelsea in 1881 was astute, as it was close to the newly-developing area of 'The Cadogans'. To match it, out came the Joubert sense of presentation – the Joubert sense of fun, best expressed in that dated word, 'Japing'. They carried out an expensive act of exhibitionism. They Frenchified the facade of 'The Pheasantry'.

They gave it the red-brick and dressed-stone look of many a seventeenth-century *manoir*. They emphasised the windows, and added balconies in the Louis XV style. In panels they listed their skills in letters incised and gilded. They enlarged the shallow house at the rear. They turned the interior into period showrooms, and devoted one to fabrics and wallpapers.

The Joubert who left the biggest mark was Felix. Trained as an architect, he was only 25 when he built Turret House for himself, in Jubilee Place. A synthesis of all the *chateaux* of the Loire, had this been sited a-top a hill, approached by darkly-forested slopes, it could have served as every child's image of the palace of *La Belle au Bois Dormant*.

Felix was sculptor, jeweller, armourer, decorator. He was also a champion fencer. He assisted in the arrangement of the display of arms at Windsor Castle.

When, in the early 1920's, the idea arose at a dinner-party of making a Dolls' House which would incorporate the finest contem-

porary craftsmanship, to be presented to Queen Mary, Sir Edwin Lutyens, the architect who designed it, wilily sent the estimates for some items to his own clients. Joubert made thirteen frames, in appropriate styles, for the State portraits, for which Mrs. Marshall Field stumped up £50, and the cradle for the night nursery set back Mr. Konig, of Tyringham, £30. From 'The Pheasantry' also came the balustrading for the garden, and Felix made one of the miniature suits of armour, and a pair of foils and fencing masks, which were his personal idea and gift.

Were Sotheby's to describe the most intriguing of these articles in a catalogue, it would read like this:

> A rare Louis XVIII style applewood cradle with ebony pin-head inlaid decoration, with ormolu and ivory mounts, the faceted octagonal tester surmounted by an ormolu crown on an ivory cushion, enclosing Prince of Wales' Feathers in ivory, the body conforming to the tester, and the pyramidal end post supporting an ormolu Guardian Angel, on eight ivory flattened bun feet. Height approx. 10.2cm, length approx. 11.5cm.

It looks as if another Joubertian joke lurked here. Felix's daughter showed me an engraved receipt, dated 1821, acknowledging a donation from 'M. Joubert' which, it said, 'would go towards Chambord'. At its head a christening is depicted. Now, in 1820, the future Charles X's son was assassinated, and *his* son, born posthumously, was heir-presumptive. In 1821, a fund was raised to purchase the Château de Chambord for this infant, who was given the title of Comte de Chambord. The Jouberts were passionately devoted to this royal family, and probably made a cradle which they would have topped off with fleurs-de-lis. Felix must have made this cot as a replica, substituting 'Prince of Wales' Feathers' for the French emblem.

It seems odd that Felix Joubert should be so little remembered in Chelsea, until one understands the reasons. He had a villa near Antibes, and when war broke out in 1939, was caught there, unable to get back. He was, however, for many years of his life, very deaf, and greatly cut off by this affliction.

The Jouberts may be said to have replaced the artisans with artists. In 1916, they acquired a truly exotic tenant who occupied the main floor until her death in 1934 – Princess Serafine Astafieva, whom the Blue Plaque commemorates. Born a Princess, she kept her own family name through two marriages, bestowing it also on her son, Slava (who died only this year). She was born in Rostov, near the mouth of the Don, in South Russia, in 1876. Her father had fought against Britain in the Crimean War; her mother was a relative of Baron Fredericks (Court Minister to Czar Nicholas II).

One of her grandfathers had married a sister of Count Leo Tolstoy, and she used to say that, as a child, she sat on his knee and pulled his beard, and he let her put snuff under his nose. When she was recovering from a serious illness, it was Tolstoy who suggested that it would help to build up her strength if she were to be taken away from the Smolny Institute and entered instead in the Imperial School of Ballet, in Theatre Street.

She graduated in 1895, and joined the company of the Maryinsky Theatre. She married a brother of Mathilde Kschessinska (who had been the mistress of the Czarevitch, later Nicholas II). Astafieva's son was about the same age as Kschessinska's by the Grand Duke Andrei. The two women always remained friends, and spent a holiday together every year on the Côte d'Azur.

By 1905, Astafieva had married again. Her second husband was a Russian of British descent, and a high official in the Russian Red Cross. Though the least domesticated of women, Serafine helped him near the front during the Russo-Japanese war, organising hospitals.

This marriage had also ended when, in 1909, Diaghilev persuaded her to join the company he was forming to show Russian Ballet in Paris for the first time. Though not a first-class dancer, she was beautiful, tall, moved well, and was an excellent mime. She took on some of the rôles created for Ida Rubinstein. When the Diaghilev Ballet first came to London in 1911, for the Coronation of King George V and Queen Mary, Astafieva took Ida's part as Cleopatra.

When war broke out in 1914, her son was in Switzerland with a tutor. Astafleva picked him up and came to England. She started a Russian Dancing Academy in a dreary drill-hall in Maiden Lane, and in 1916 moved it into 'The Pheasantry'. Her teaching was recognised from the start as outstanding. She offered general classes as well as ballet, and among her pupils were June (later Lady Inverclyde) and a pretty child called Marjorie Robertson, who became famous as Anna Neagle. (When Dame Anna's husband, Herbert Wilcox, decided to make a film about Nell Gwynn, it was his own idea to invite Astafieva to create dances for it.)

Diaghilev returned to London in September 1918, and became a frequent visitor at 'The Pheasantry', dropping in to salute Astafieva and drink tea. (He had many friends in Chelsea; including the Sitwells.) He took her two star pupils into his company – first Anton Dolin, and, before her fifteenth birthday, Alicia Marks, who was to become Dame Alicia Markova. The third star from 'The Pheasantry' nest had spent only one year there when Astafieva died. She was Peggy Hookham, later known as Dame Margot Fonteyn.

A pupil who did not seek to become a performer was Arnold Haskell, who was to become the first Director of the Royal Ballet School, and whose mother, Emmy, modelled a delightful head of Astafieva of which two casts were made in bronze, presumably by Joubert. Sir Arnold has one, and Astafieva's pianist, Ronnie Longville, entrusted her copy to me to give to the Theatre Museum. Emmy used to bring down gorgeous hampers crammed with goodies so that everyone could feast! (Usually they all had lunch at a café a few doors away, run by Ada Reeve's sister, and they also favoured the Unity, opposite.)

Diaghilev used the studio for rehearsals, and Massine worked in it on his ballets, including *La Boutique Fantasque* and *Le Tricorne*. Robert Sielle, the framer, was an exhibition dancer with Annette Mills, and often rented the studio for practice. He would ask Astafieva to think up new routines; perhaps they sought guidance in the teatime sessions he recalled, when everyone clustered into the small sitting-room. The tea-leaves had to be read, and out came the ouija-board. There was plenty of hard work, but a *vie de bohème*, too. (And all the other studios were occupied by artists.)

Astafieva had beautiful legs, and usually wore white tights – and always a bandeau. She could look like a hippie, or the epitome of elegance. She was wildly generous, and would give a rich jewel – whilst she still possessed any – to the teller of a hard-luck story. At the end of a lesson, she would say, "Those who can – pay!" Of one fact she was proud. "I was never a refugee. I was already here, earning a living. I started my Academy with sixpence."

Astafieva wasn't a saint, but her personality had great richness. Perhaps it is just as well that she didn't care a fig for material possessions, otherwise she might haunt those who have desecrated 'The Pheasantry'.

1976

Note: In 2004 the 'Pheasantry' has a new life as part of the Pizza Express chain. It has been sympathetically restored and the dancers' *barre* is still to be seen upstairs in the mirror'd dining room.

SIR JOHN SOANE AND THE ROYAL HOSPITAL

—

Dorothy Stroud

On Saturday 7 February, 1807, John Soane noted in his pocketbook 'S. Wyatt died this day'. In fact, Samuel Wyatt's death came very suddenly while putting on his boots. He had, among his many other posts and an extensive private practise, acted for fifteen years as Clerk of the Works to the Royal Hospital, Chelsea, an office in which he had succeeded Robert Adam. Soane is therefore not likely to have given any thought to the Chelsea Clerkship until he heard of Wyatt's demise, but once this occurred, he seems to have acted swiftly towards obtaining it for himself, and it is significant that an entry in his note-book records on Sunday 15 February that he had ridden 'with Mrs. S. to Chelsea.' His application proved successful, and on 4 March he was at the Hospital to meet various officials, while a week later he called on the Governor, Sir David Dundas, from whom he received the warrant for his appointment.

From then on the Hospital was to claim a considerable amount of Soane's working time. His salary was £200 a year, with an allowance of three shillings a day 'table money' (the equivalent of subsistence money), and a small house in which he was supposed to reside. On 30 June he noted that he had 'slept at Chelsea first time', but a drawing of the house shows it as a mean little dwelling at that time, and probably it was Mrs. Soane's reluctance to leave their comfortable home in Lincoln's Inn Fields, and join her husband there, which prompted his request to the Lords Commissioners six months later to be excused from regular residence at Chelsea. Over the ensuing years, however, he was able partly to rebuild and extend the house, and it is evident that after Mrs. Soane's death in 1815 he came to regard it as a haven to which he could escape from sad memories in Lincoln's Inn Fields.

For the first two years Soane's work was mainly concerned with routine repairs to such items as chimneys, cornices and roofs. Stone sills were introduced below the windows of the main block facing north, and the brickwork of this façade was repointed. Maintenance was, of course, to be a recurrent problem, but in 1809 came the first of Soane's major undertakings which may briefly be listed as

the New Infirmary (1809-12), the stables (1814-17), the Bake House (1814) and the Gardener's House (1816), all of which were in or adjacent to the West Road. The new Secretary's Office (1818) and the Physician's House (1819) were both on the East Road, but the Surgeon's House (1821) was on the West Road.

The building of a new infirmary had been a matter of discussion for several years. By 1809 it had eventually been decided to select a site on part of which stood Yarborough House of which a portion was to be retained in the new building. This house had originally been the modest dwelling used by Sir Robert Walpole after taking the office of Paymaster General in 1714. It was later enlarged by Vanbrugh and was then taken by Lord Yarborough whose name it subsequently bore. Of Soane's many proposals for the Infirmary that finally selected by the Chelsea Board consisted of a long range of buildings running from east to west, with two wings extending to the south. At the east end of the main block, and extending into that wing, were the parts of Yarborough House which were retained, including the old drawing-room with a coffered ceiling and marble chimneypiece. The external walls of the new building were of stock brick and carried a Portland stone entablature of Soanic ingenuity, with patera set between token *triglyphs*. On the south the theme of semi-circular brick arches in which the windows were set was continued to form an open loggia connecting the two wings, while on the north projected a single-storey, five-window bay. The Infirmary was ready to receive its furnishings by the end of 1812, the building costs having by this time amounted to just over £28, 135. Unhappily it was destroyed by bombs in the last war, and the site is now covered by the National Army Museum.

The next building of note was the replacement of the Wren stables with a more compact block, Soane's design for which proved to be one of his most idiosyncratic compositions. In this the stables and coach-houses are grouped round a courtyard the entrance to which is through the centre bay of a rectangular block in stock brick. On either side are doors leading to staff lodgings, both the doors and the central entrance being set in large round-headed brick recesses. The first floor rooms of the lodgings receive light from windows on the courtyard side, and the staircases are lit from the north and south walls. The simplicity of the main façade of the stable block is typical of Soane's fondness for stripping away all non-essentials, the only concession to decoration here being a recessed panel over the central arch, and the token *triglyphs* of the cornice here contrived with up-ended bricks. Although shaken by a

The Smoking House at Chelsea

blast in the war-time raid which destroyed the Infirmary, the stables survived, and are practically unchanged.

For the new Bake House which Soane was asked to build in 1814, and for two or three other small buildings which followed, Soane kept to the style used by Wren for such single-storey quarters, that is, brick walls with stone quoins and steeply projecting eaves to the slate roofs. The same style was also adopted for the facade of the third of his major buildings, the new Secretary's Office on the East Road designed in 1818. Inside, however, are rooms of typically Soanic simplicity, the main door opening into a spacious hall with offices on either side. It is crossed at its further end by a narrow corridor running the entire length of the building and giving access to further offices, a library and a waiting room. At the far end of the hall hangs the large painting of the Battle of Waterloo by George Jones, from whom Soane was some years later to commission a painting showing the interior of *The Smoking House at Chelsea*, a small building which he erected at the north end of the West Road in 1829, and which was later turned into a guard-house after the rules on smoking in the Hospital had become less stringent. The painting still hangs in Soane's house in Lincoln's Inn Fields. The furnishing of the Secretary's Office was carried out under Soane's direction in 1819 and much of it remains *in situ*.

Also surviving, and again remarkable for its simplicity, is the little garden shelter in the south-east area of the grounds. Here brick piers with retracted necking support a pitched roof which was originally thatched, but is now slated. No drawings for it seem to have survived, but the Hospital records show that it was constructed from one of four designs which Soane submitted to the Board in 1834. It was, therefore, the last of Soane's works at the Royal Hospital for he died in January 1837, and with his death the office of Clerk of the Works came to an end. [1980]

Royal Hospital: Stable, Infirmary and Clerk-of-the-Works house

DOWN THE KING'S ROAD –
BUT ONLY BY ROYAL PERMISSION

Simon Bendall

The King's Private Road, which was the route from St. James's Palace to Hampton Court, dates back to the third decade of the seventeenth century. In 1626 Thomas Hebbs, Surveyor of the Kings Highways, published an order "to take care of the repair of the way leading from Chelsea to Fulham." At this time the way crossed the brook called the West Bourne, which flowed in the Thames just east of the Royal Hospital, at Stone Bridge and then ran along what is now the line of Royal Hospital Road.

It was not until the reign of Charles II that the route was shortened to run across the Five Fields, where Eaton Square now stands, crossing the West Bourne at Bloody Bridge, a site which is now slightly east of Sloane Square (built in 1771), and following the current line of the King's Road to Fulham. At this time the road ran through fields and market gardens since the village of Chelsea lay further south on the Thames.

In the reign of Charles II there was at least one gate across the King's Road (at Town End, where Church Street crosses), and possibly others. At this period the gate was shut after the seeds had been sown on the surrounding land and not reopened until after harvest. By 1711 six gates had been erected across the road. They were at the back of Buckingham House, (now Buckingham Palace); "over against Chelsea College", (then and now the Chelsea Royal Hospital); Chelsea Lane End (now where Church Street crosses the King's Road); World's End; Sandy End (now by the Palmerston pub where the King's Road joins the New King's Road by Waterford Rd); and at Fulham.

By this time the road was in such a poor state as a result of the waggons of market gardeners taking their produce to London, that for the next three years it seems to have been unused and the gates kept locked while the road was "mending and settling". The local freeholders and their tenants along the road apparently "found another way very quietly".

By 1719, the road was obviously in use again but the locals were finding it hard to use since in the intervening period they were apparently forbidden to do so. In that year they petitioned the Commissioners of His Majesty's Treasury to recover "their immemorial custom, use and possession (for we were never denied a passage till late)". They pointed out that while it had been reported that up to 48 carts a night used the road, they must belong to "foreigners" since the parish only had seven carts that used the route. They seem to have been successful judging by the reply: "My Lords direct Mr. Watkins to permit the tenants of the lands adjoining to the King's Road, through Chelsea, to have free passage through the same, with their carts and horses, in the manner which they have been accustomed to." The six gatekeepers also petitioned for payment of three years work on the road and on the 22 February 1722/3 it was agreed that they would be paid £5 per annum. The King's Road remained the King's Private Road until Christmas 1829 when the Commissioners of Woods and Forests, who at this time had the responsibility for its upkeep, gave up their rights and it then became a public road.

Before that time, the use of the road had been a privilege for which special passes were necessary. There were four types and all bear Georgian monograms and two types are dated. There is only one, genuine official die for each type. The first type was probably introduced in 1722/3 as a result of the need to recoup the £30 p.a. paid to the six gatekeepers and possibly to pay for future repairs. I presume that the passes were issued to local landlords and tenants for a modest fee and others who used the road would pay more in tolls.

It has been suggested that these passes were key tags but this seems unlikely for two reasons; firstly, because it was surely not possible to manufacture six locks in the early eighteenth century so accurately that one key would fit all six locks and unlikely also that each tag had six keys attached. Secondly, we know that the gates were kept locked from time to time, and since the gatekeepers would have had to open the gates for those without keys, presumably on payment, why go to the trouble of issuing hundreds of keys when the gatekeeper could have opened the gate on production of a pass. It seems that pedestrians could walk the road freely but that the gates and passes were intended only for wheeled traffic.

The writer has studied fifty specimens of the four types. Of these, 27 are in private collections, ten in trade, eleven in the British Museum and two in the Chelsea Public Library. These were composed of eleven specimens of type I, 27 of type II, eleven of type III and one of type IV. Type I is cast in brass, types II and III struck in copper and type IV apparently struck only in silver. There were many forgeries of all the first three types. Since the first type was cast (No. 1), it must have been comparatively easy to copy them by casting. Thus it is only possible to confirm that a pass is false when it is not cast from an official original. Using this criteria, 36% of the specimens studied were copies. This obviously posed a problem which must certainly have been the reason why in 1731 the first struck type was introduced (No. 2). Although the second type was struck from dies it was also copied extensively. The copies were also struck but because of the inferior workmanship of the forgers, the copies they made are easier to detect today. Some 60% of the 27 specimens examined are false.

It is, no doubt, because of the large number of the forgeries of this second type that only six years later another type was introduced. This was also struck but in an oval shape and, for extra

security, numbered (No. 3). On the passes examined, the lowest number was 36 and the highest 1388. On most of the passes there is a die flaw at 9 o'clock on the obverse, which indicates that part of the die broke off after only a small number of passes had been struck. It was obviously not considered worth engraving a new die so the majority of passes struck have the flaw. It is also obvious that the complete issue of passes was struck before being numbered since numbers 36 and 1388 are the only two without the flaw whereas numbers 71, 503, 538, 696, 750, 975 and 1070 are flawed.

Of the eleven specimens examined only two are false. As with the previous type, the forgeries are die struck and also numbered. A further indication of the fact that most of the genuine passes exhibited the die flaw is the fact that the forgers also engraved the flaw on their die. Many of the copper passes are quite worn which would indicate a long life. The last type (No. 4) is struck in silver and may not even be genuine. Some years ago I was told that they were probably forgeries by W. C. Wells who was working from the turn of the century until his death in 1948. The British Museum do not have a specimen and it was unknown to Benjamin Nightingale who collected and wrote on tickets and passes in the mid-nineteenth century. The earliest record I have is of the sale of one in the 1920's. The specimen illustrated here has an early nineteenth century look to it and is engraved with the name of Lord Grenville. He was Ranger and Keeper of St. James's and Green Parks until 1794. He was a noted politician and supporter of William Wilberforce and the son of the Chancellor of the Exchequer who had introduced the Stamp Duty which helped lead to the American War of Independence. Although he did not die until 1834, he suffered a stroke in 1824 and retired to his country house, Dropmore, Bucks. The pass, if genuine, must therefore have been issued before 1824. I have been told of another pass of this type named to the Duke of Bedford.

1995

THE CARLYLES AT CHEYNE ROW

Peter Quennell

The marriage of Jane and Thomas Carlyle, solemnized in October, 1826, lasted until 1866, and before they plighted their troth, both husband and wife had expressed the deepest hesitations. "Without great sacrifices on both sides", Carlyle had written, "the possibility of our union is an empty dream"; while Jane had declared in 1823, "Your Friend I will be… but your Wife! Never, never!"

To some extent the obstacle they confronted was social and economic. Jane was "an ex-spoilt child", brought up by an adoring mother in Scottish middle-class society, well educated, attractive, equally proud, we are told, of her Latin and her eyelashes; whereas Carlyle's father was a rustic stonemason who had later taken up farming. Thomas had made himself a historian and a writer by dint of his own laborious efforts, but in the process he had ruined his health and suffered perpetually from dyspepsia, insomnia, and a host of nervous ills. Jane admired him, but felt that she could not love him.

Yet the rough peasant-scholar and the volatile middle-class girl had somehow drifted into marriage, and as a middle-aged woman, Jane would write to a favourite cousin, explaining what she thought had happened: "In virtue of his being *the least unlikable* man in the place, I let him dance attendance on my young person, till I came to *need* him – all the same as my slippers to go to a ball in, or my bonnet to go out to walk. When I finally agreed to marry him, I *cried* excessively and felt excessively shocked – but if I had then said *no* he would have left me."

For the first few years of their marriage, she accepted the consequences of her decision bravely. In 1828 they moved from Edinburgh to the lonely farm of Craigenputtock, where the silence was so profound that they could often hear sheep cropping in the field outside. During the winter months, a deeper hush descended, and the snow piled up against the door: when they opened it, a mountainous drift would sweep like an avalanche across the flagstones of the kitchen.

Finally, in 1834, Carlyle having at last published *Sartor Resartus*, they felt rich enough to move south. The London house they chose was Number 5 Great Cheyne Row (today Number 24 Cheyne Row), a largish Queen Anne house close to the river Thames, which at that period still retained the muddy fore-shore that Whistler and Walter Greaves painted, where barges and sailing boats lay beached on its verge, amid decrepit wharves and ramshackle wooden jetties. They were to spend the rest of their lives in that house. There Jane Carlyle's body was brought after her sudden death in 1866; and there, an embittered, disconsolate sage, Carlyle died in 1881.

For me the long years they spent at Cheyne Row have a special interest. I am their next-door neighbour, and rarely a day passes when I am not somehow reminded of them. Chelsea itself has changed. It is no longer a secluded suburb, full of trees and ancient houses; late-Victorian buildings have swamped the "hawthorn lanes", meadows, and market gardens that once extended beyond the King's Road toward Kensington and Knightsbridge.

Yet Cheyne Row keeps much of its quietude, and the Carlyles' house preserves its cloistral, somewhat gloomy atmosphere. Most of the changes it has undergone since it was erected in the year 1708 – by a speculative builder who had bought up the bowling green of a demolished manor house – were made by the Carlyles themselves. Jane was no respecter of early eighteenth-century panelling. Perhaps because she liked to think of herself as modern, or because she identified the depression that Carlyle frequently radiated with the sombre background of their old-fashioned house, or perhaps because she dreaded the bugs that often hid behind antique wood-work, she removed the panelling from many walls and substituted, if she could afford it, prettily flowered wallpaper.

From Number 26 Cheyne Row, our view of the Carlyles' house is particularly absorbing. Just below, as we look to the right across an antiquated red-brick wall, lies the strip of garden where Carlyle, on summer evenings, used to smoke his clay pipe, which he stored in a crevice between the bricks. A photograph taken in 1857, shows him seated near the garden door, wearing the tall-crowned, large-brimmed black hat that shadowed his then grey-bearded visage; little Nero, Jane's dog, is comfortably spread-eagled beside his chair. Nero, who is buried in the garden, was an important member of the Carlyle household and appears in a series of dramatic tales. There was one occasion, Jane relates, when the intrepid animal tried to fly:

'For a first attempt his success was not so bad... and tho' he *did* plash down on the pavement at the feet of an astonished Boy he broke no bones, was only quite *stunned*.... It was after breakfast,

and he had been standing at the open window, watching the birds – one of his chief delights – while Elizabeth was "dusting out" for Mr. C. Lying in my bed, I heard thro' the deal partition Elizabeth scream; "oh God! oh Nero!" and rush downstairs like a strong wind out at the street door. I sat up in my bed aghast – waiting with a feeling as of the Heavens falling till I heard her reascending the stairs and then I sprang to meet her in my night shift. She was white as a sheet, ready to faint... "Is he killed?" I asked... Mr. C. came down from his bedroom with his chin all over soap and asked, "has anything happened to Nero?" "Oh Sir he *must* have broken *all* his legs, he leapt out at *your* window!" "God bless me! "said Mr. C. and returned to finish his shaving.'

His mistress adored him, and his master valued his company. Nero regularly followed Carlyle on his long crepuscular walks through Chelsea – "little dim-white speck of Life, of Love, Fidelity and Feeling; girdled by the Darkness of Night Eternal" – while the sage meditated, as he trudged the streets, upon the evils of the modern world and his own forlorn existence, or thought of the sleepless hours that awaited him once he had plodded back to his solitary bed.

In the same photograph, a clump of bushes and a small tree occupy the right-hand side. They conceal a homely domestic office. From our upper windows we look down upon a modest flat-roofed structure. This is the household privy. The Carlyles, while they occupied Number 5, had no kind of interior sanitation; and as both of them seem to have suffered from perpetually disordered livers, and Carlyle was constantly being dispatched to the chemist's shop in search of the powerful laxative called "blue pills," the fact that they had only an unheated outdoor privy on wet and windy London days must have caused them much acute discomfort.

Another odd thought is how many of the Carlyles' troubles originated in the house we now inhabit. For them it was an almost legendary place, peopled by a series of demonic families whose principal purpose, so far as Jane could make out, was to prevent Carlyle from writing. The earliest, a rather genteel family called Lambert, arrived in 1839. With them, alas, they had brought a parrot, which, when they carried it into the garden, screeched under Carlyle's window, so that he "fairly sprang to his feet, declaring he could 'neither think nor live'." Jane then composed a diplomatic note, and the parrot was removed.

Worse came when one of the Misses Lambert started taking music lessons, both vocal and instrumental. Carlyle was working then on the first floor, and only a thin wall divided him from the sitting room – it is still our sitting room – that the Misses Lambert used. His patience was limited; his hatred of any kind of noise had already developed into an obsession; and one morning he suddenly left his table, seized the poker, and delivered a couple of tremendous blows on the wall "exactly opposite where he fancied the young Lady seated". The deep silence that followed lasted "for the next twelve hours". But neither this drastic action nor a polite exchange of notes could quite subdue the Misses Lambert, and intermittent "squallings" and tinklings continued to torment Carlyle – he was then toiling at *Past and Present* and his monumental book on Oliver Cromwell – throughout 1842 and 1843.

Even worse than the musical Lamberts were some of the families who succeeded them – the Roncas, a bohemian Irish family who, besides noisily carpentering in the back garden and hanging out their squalid household laundry, kept a parrot, dogs, and chickens. After much diplomacy and some stern threats, they were at last reduced to order. But then in 1865, the year before Jane's death, another fearful blow descended. The latest tenant, "a very mysterious 'dressmaker', " seemed a retiring, inoffensive person. But she had lodgers who proved to be more troublesome, and early one morning Mrs. Carlyle made a hideous discovery. As she wrote in a letter on December 25:

'For years back there has reigned over all these gardens a heavenly quiet – thanks to my heroic exertions in exterminating nuisances… Figure then my horror, my despair, on being waked one dark morning with the crowing of a cock, that seemed to issue from under my bed!… I lay with my heart in my mouth… listening for Mr. C.'s foot stamping frantically, as of old… and there was a sight to see – a ragged, *irish*-looking hen house… and sauntering to and fro nine goodly hens, and a stunning cock!'

Once again she managed to intervene and arranged "that the cock should be shut up in a cellar… from three in the afternoon till ten in the morning", by which time Mr. C. would have retired to the dismal soundproof room that he had now had built on the top floor. Jane, whose character evidently included a certain touch of masochism, must somehow have relished such domestic dramas. She had thought of writing a novel, she admitted, about the "mysteries" of Number 6, and used to amuse her friend Charles Dickens with the curious stories she told him of the house and its inhabitants. Dickens believed that they would make an excellent book. He had always admired her gifts – "none of the writing women

T. Carlyle

came near her at all", he said, and as a man who enjoyed the companionship of the opposite sex, he found her more than usually attractive. Not only, noted his biographer John Forster, did Mrs. Carlyle entertain him, she inspired a deeper sentiment: "there was something beyond, beyond" – an element of physical and emotional sympathy.

Indeed, long after she had lost her looks and had become elderly and gaunt and haggard, Jane was still charming, and many of the distinguished men who presented themselves at Number 5 Cheyne Row arrived to visit Jane alone. Both the Italian patriot Giuseppe Mazzini and the French exile Godefroy Cavaignac (one of the leaders of the left wing under Charles X and Louis Philippe) had undoubtedly conceived a romantic affection for their hostess, and their love was, to some extent, returned. She also had the adoration of the aging Leigh Hunt, who, with his untidy children and his feckless and difficult wife, lived in Upper Cheyne Row around the corner.

Marianne Hunt, whom Byron had once so cordially detested, had apparently taken to the bottle, and the Hunts, led an improvident and harassed existence. Hunt – "a pretty man, " Carlyle remembered, "...with the airiest kindly style of sparkling talk" – often took refuge at Number 5 from the squalid confusion of his own home. "He would lean on his elbow against the mantelpiece... and look around him... before taking leave for the night: 'as if I were a *Lar*', said he once, 'or permanent Household God here!'

...Another time, rising from this *Lar* attitude, he repeated (voice very fine) as if in sport of parody, yet with something of very sad perceptible: 'While I to sulphurous and penal fire' – as the last thing before vanishing." Among Hunt's best-known poems is the graceful triolet "Jenny Kissed Me", which he addressed to Jane when she had surprised him by jumping from her chair to throw her arms around him as he entered.

Both the Carlyles, despite their quirks and prejudices, were fond of entertaining newcomers. Since the publication of *Sartor Resartus*, Carlyle had become a literary lion, and Jane, for all her caustic asides, was pleased to see "the host of my husband's lady admirers" gathered about him in her presence. There was Harriet Martineau, the famous political economist, holding out her ear trumpet "with a pretty blushing air of coquetry", and later, the novelist Geraldine Jewsbury, lying on the carpet at the great man's feet.

Nor were the Carlyles averse to fashionable society, though Jane often criticized its arrogance and extravagance. She records in a letter to her mother, written on 7 April 1839, that a week previously "the sound of a whirlwind rushed thro' the street', and there stopt with a prancing of steeds and footman thunder at this door, an equipage, all resplendent with sky-blue and silver... whence emanated Count d'Orsay". The renowned exquisite had behaved in a particularly gracious manner, while his host, never easy to impress, had displayed a solid homespun dignity.

'A sight it was to make one think the millennium actually at hand, when the lion and the lamb, and all incompatible things

The Carlyles' House, Cheyne Row

should consort together. Carlyle in his grey plaid suit... looking blandly at the Prince of Dandies; and the Prince of Dandies on an opposite chair, all resplendent as a diamond-beetle, looking blandly at *him*. D'Orsay is a really handsome man, after one has heard him speak and found that he has both wit and sense; but at first sight his beauty is of that rather disgusting sort which seems to be like genius "of no sex". And this impression is greatly helped by the fantastical finery of his dress; sky-blue satin cravat, yards of gold chain, with white French gloves, light drab greatcoat lined with velvet of the same colour, invisible inexpressibles, skin-coloured and fitting like a glove.'

Number 5 was seldom a dull house yet during the last twenty years of the Carlyles' occupation, their life was darkly overshadowed. As early as 1846 Jane had begun to doubt whether she still retained her husband's love; and in the 1850's she could not help acknowledging that Mr. C., who had previously appeared indifferent to all women "*as women*", had developed a Platonic infatuation for a famous London hostess, the Junonian Lady Ashburton, and often willingly deserted Cheyne Row to spend his evenings in her company. Meanwhile Jane's health was gradually breaking down, undermined by the enormous doses of henbane and morphia that, as a remedy for her chronic sleeplessness, she had been taking night after night since she reached the age of forty-five. Sometimes she feared she might be going mad, and in 1863 a minor street accident resulted in months of excruciating pain.

It was a disastrous marriage – that is at least the conclusion we draw from the Carlyles' letters. James Anthony Froude, a close friend and the author of a four volume biography that appeared between 1882 and 1884, asserts that it was never consummated; and certainly Jane exhibited many of the traits of a disappointed and embittered woman whose emotional grievances found vent in a long succession of psychosomatic maladies. Yet was she quite so miserable as she often liked to pretend? Though she would speak of "the Valley of the Shadow of Marriage" and expatiate at length upon her daily woes, both the Carlyles, we must remember, possessed a keen dramatic sense.

For them their checkered married life was an absorbing tragicomedy. Carlyle needed something to grumble about, apart from the current evils of society and the general turpitude of modern mankind, while Jane required a constant supply of subjects on which she could exercise her sharp-edged wit. As a born novelist who had failed to write a book, she may have half enjoyed their misadventures. Her references to her remarkable husband are sometimes tartly disparaging, even downright acrimonious. Yet it is clear not only that she admired him, but that he had aroused in her a

deep devotion, a feeling that soon transcended any youthful dreams of ordinary human happiness.

Both were proud, and both were lonely. During what Carlyle afterward called their "sore life-pilgrimage", they became inseparable fellow travellers. Jane, however, did not cease to fret against his atrabilious egotism – when she was angry, observed a critical acquaintance, she had "a tongue like a cat's, which would take the skin off at a touch" – and her husband was generally far too busy to give her the attention she demanded. Not until he had finally lost her, and had opened her private papers, did he begin to understand her secret sufferings.

Thus the long marriage of Jane and Thomas Carlyle was neither happy nor unhappy. Although its moments of desperate wretchedness probably outnumbered its occasional hours of sunshine, Jane's earliest letters, in which she addresses Carlyle as her "Goody, Goody, dear Goody" and promises him – she is staying at her mother's house – "to make it all up to you in kisses" when she returns to Craigenputtock, are scarcely more affectionate in tone than the last she ever posted. Written on April 21 1866, this letter is headed simply "Dearest."

That afternoon, she drove through Hyde Park, taking a friend's little dog, and when she put it out for a run, it was knocked over by a passing carriage. She dismounted and, finding that it was unhurt, told the coachman to complete their journey. But later he noticed that she was sitting motionless, her hands, "palm uppermost the right hand, reverse way the left", lying quietly upon her lap. She was dead, killed by a heart seizure; and her body was presently carried back to Cheyne Row, to the bed with red hangings she had inherited from her mother and in which she had herself been born. Today, the house that the Carlyles occupied still has a hushed and solemn air, but both its custodians have assured me that they have never felt that it was haunted; nor does the smallest spectral influence extend to the adjacent "house of mysteries". I have listened in vain for the sound of Thomas Carlyle's poker thundering against the sitting-room wall.

1981

LEIGH HUNT 1784–1859

Jane Dorrell

Leigh Hunt was the son of an American lawyer whose unfortunate timing in supporting the Union in 1775 led to his deportation from America. He arrived, penniless, in England in 1776 and unable to practise law, was ordained as a preacher. James Henry Leigh was born in 1784. He was educated at Christ's Hospital, a Bluecoat boy. He won a literary prize when he was 15, and two years later after his father published his *Juvenilia* he started his career in journalism with a job on his brother John's newspaper, the *News*, the first of many joint ventures. In 1808 they founded the *Examiner*, a liberal paper which attracted Byron, Shelley and Lamb. Unfortunately it also attracted the attention of the establishment and in 1812 both brothers were convicted of seditious libel against the Prince Regent and sentenced to two years' imprisonment. Leigh Hunt soon sweet-talked himself into ground floor rooms in the prison infirmary which he decorated in rose-patterned wallpaper and furnished with books. There was a little garden outside where he would stroll with his visitors – Jeremy Bentham, the Lambs and Hazlitt. 'There was bustling talk and merriment', said Byron.

In 1809 after a tempestuous courtship he had married Marian Kent who was described as 'childlike and unable to follow his conversation' though she did manage to give him eleven children. In 1816 he was the first to publish Keats which brought him lasting fame but his liberal views continued to be unacceptable in England and he went to Italy in 1822 to join Shelley, arriving, with appalling timing just a few days before the poet drowned. The Hunts then moved to Pisa to stay with Byron. The latter was not amused by the influx of this menagerie into his palazzo – there

Leigh Hunt, age 17

were now seven children in tow – and the family moved to Florence. Three years later, destitute, they returned to England.

In 1822 he published *Lord Byron and Some of his Contempories* and it was upon this that his reputation was founded. In 1833 he moved to the 'cheap and unfashionable locality of Chelsea' – around the corner from Thomas Carlyle who said of him : 'His Household disclosed itself to be huggermugger, unthrift and sordid collapse'. Jane Carlyle was infuriated by Mrs Hunt's constant scrounging but the affectionate welcome she gave Leigh Hunt inspired his enchanting lines:

At age 36

Jenny kissed me when we met
Jumping from the chair she sat in;
Time, you thief, who love to get
Sweets into your list, put that in;
Say I'm weary, say I'm sad,
Say that health and wealth have missed me,
Say I'm growing old but add,
Jenny kissed me.

In his last years he became a 'literary tourist attraction'. He had walked and talked with Byron, Keats and Shelley. Dickens portrayed him – unkindly – as Skimpole in 'Bleak House', and a bust which shows him as (Carlyle's description) 'a pretty man' stands today in Keats's house in Hampstead.

1996

At age 66

THE LIFE AND TIMES OF SIR HANS SLOANE

Richard Ballard

Sir Hans Sloane was one of the great shakers and movers of Old Chelsea; physician, property developer, discoverer of the medicinal qualities of milk chocolate, facilitator of herbalists, natural philosopher and collector. Alexander Pope's lines, 'Butterflies for Sloane', show him well known as a polymath in his lifetime. Living between the Renaissance and the Enlightenment, he regarded no human concern foreign to his mind. The colossal aspect of Sloane is well presented in Rysbrach's statue of him which is now in the British Museum. (Copies are in the Chelsea Physic Garden and Sloane Square.)

As you approach Chelsea Old Church going westwards along Cheyne Walk, one of its significant features takes your eye: the monument to Sir Hans Sloane in the south-east corner of the churchyard. It is the work of Joseph Wilton RA (1717-18O3) with a classical funeral urn and the entwined serpents that have been symbols of the medical profession since Hippocrates's time. On the south face of the monument is the inscription which reads:

> 'To the memory of Sir Hans Sloane Bart, President of the Royal Society and of the College of Physicians, who in the year of our Lord 1753, the 92nd year of his age, without the least pain of body and with a conscious serenity of mind, ended a virtuous and beneficent life. This monument was erected by his two daughters Eliza Cadogan and Sarah Stanley.'

Though no-one is on oath in lapidary inscriptions, as Wilton's friend, Dr Johnson, remarked, a review of Sloane's life bears out the truth of this one. If hard work and scientific acumen are the marks of virtue, then he was virtuous, and the existence of the British Museum and the core of treasures within it, together with the Chelsea Physic Garden, are witnesses to his beneficence. Sloane was a receiver-general of taxes, and his mother was the daughter of Dr Hicks, who had been chaplain to Archbishop Laud. When he was sixteen Hans suffered from a condition called haemoptysis and he never again drank wine or spirits. Soon afterwards he went to France, studying medicine in Paris and Montpellier. He learned botany under the guidance of celebrated teachers, Magnol and Tournefort, and received his degree as a Doctor of Medicine from the University of Orange in 1683. He was in England the year after and made friends with prominent scientists like Ray and Boyle, becoming a Fellow of the Royal Society himself in 1685. Two years later he was admitted to the College of Physicians and then he crossed the Atlantic to join the staff of the Duke of Albemarle, the Governor of Jamaica, as his physician.

When he returned to London in May 1689, he brought specimens of eight hundred West Indian plants with him for study. He set up his medical practice in Bloomsbury Square and, from 1689 until 1712, was Secretary of the Royal Society.

Oxford University made him MD in 1701. His book about the natural history of the West Indies was eventually published in two volumes in 1707 and 1725. He was recognised as a European figure, becoming a foreign member of the French Society of Sciences and of the Imperial Academy of St Petersburg, recently set up by Peter the Great. At home he received recognition as President of the College of Physicians in 1719 and held the office until 1735. On the death of Sir Isaac Newton in 1727 he became President of the Royal Society as well and remained such until his retirement in 1741. Earlier, Queen Anne had consulted him as a physician, and he was authorised to inoculate members of the royal family. 1722 saw him as Physician-General to the Army. His baronetcy dates from 1716, and in 1727 he was appointed First Physician to King George II. He was in charge of Christ's Hospital for thirty-six years between 1694 and 1730. When the colony of Georgia was floated in 1732 as a place for discharged convicts, Sloane was one of those who promoted it under General Oglethorpe, its first Governor.

In the midst of all this activity he bought Chelsea Manor in 1712, paying £2,500 to the second Lord Cheyne for it, but he did not retire to settle there until 1741. The oldest botanical garden still existing had been in Chelsea since 1673, when the Apothecaries' Company took out a 61-year lease at five pounds a year from the then Lord of the Manor, Charles Cheyne, on land around space for building a boat-house for their state barge. The following year this land was planted with herbs, which were added to the next year by herbs from a similar garden in Westminster. The Apothecaries' Company lease had only twelve years to run in 1722. For the same rent, and for supplying the Royal Society with specimens of 'fifty distinct plants, well dried and preserved' from the

garden each year, with an agreement that the acreage should be put to no other use than that for which they held it, Sloane granted the land to the Apothecaries' Company in perpetuity, thus obviating the need for them to lease it to one of their members for a short time in return for a salary, which had meant that it did not reach its potential. Previously there had been some animosity towards Sloane on the part of individuals in the Apothecaries' Company because he had been promoting a scheme to set up free dispensaries of medicines for poor people which would have deprived them of income. After he had granted them the land in perpetuity for no extra rent, they saw him in a different light and eleven years later, in 1733, decided to put up a marble statue of him in the garden. This was the one sculpted by Michael Rysbrach. It was finished in 1737 and cost £80. Originally it was in front of the greenhouse but it was moved to the centre of the garden in 1748.

Six years after his return from Jamaica Sloane had married the widow of Fulk Rose, a landowner in the colony, whose fortune helped him to establish himself. In his last years in Chelsea he had more time for his extensive collection. In 1749, when he was eighty-eight, he bequeathed his collections to the nation on condition that his family was paid £20,000, which was agreed by an Act of Parliament in the year of his death, with Horace Walpole as a trustee. The year after, Montagu House was bought to house them, together with Cotton's and Harley's manuscript collections. Smirke's great Bloomsbury building followed fifty years later.

2003

THE ROYAL MILITARY ASYLUM

William Dorrell

Above the grand tetrastyle portico of the Duke of York's Head-quarters in Chelsea there was once written in stone:

THE ROYAL MILITARY ASYLUM FOR THE CHILDREN OF
SOLDIERS OF THE REGULAR ARMY

The Asylum was conceived 200 years ago when, in 1799, Parliament ratified a bill put before the Commons by William Windham, Secretary at War, for building and maintaining a boarding school for the orphans of British soldiers. The proposed site was close to the Royal Hospital so that, as Windham remarked, 'both ends of a soldier's life would meet; in the one they would find asylum in their infancy, and in the other a retreat in their old age'. He asked for £25,000 but by 1801, when the foundation stone was laid by the Duke of York, Parliament had agreed to pay the full cost of the building and granted £24,000 a year to run it.

The Asylum was designed to take 700 boys and 300 girls. The Duke of York laid the foundation stone in 1801 and its doors opened to the first 200 pupils in 1803. The Duke was an active patron who was popular with the children and he remained a frequent visitor for the rest of his life.

The Asylum is built of London stock brick and Portland stone in a plain Georgian style with a tetrastyle portico of the Tuscan order. As Pevsner observes, 'The combination of austerity and dignity is wholly successful'. The building, which is listed Grade II, was designed by John Sanders (1768-1826), the first of Sir John Soane's pupils who, over the next 20 years, went on to build over 200 barracks and make his fortune. The cost of buildings and land was £104, 187 4s 2d. The land was originally leased for 78 years from Lord Cadogan, whose seat had once been here. The Asylum governors were later able to buy the freehold. Behind the central building was a laundry and in 1810 an infirmary was built beside it which was attended by some distinguished physicians including, at the time of an outbreak of ophthalmia, the King's oculist. The

Asylum workshops were originally built along the King's Road but in 1865 these were demolished to make way for shops and were replaced by the present building behind the north wing.

In 1835 a chapel was built in the north-west corner of the grounds and, in 1855, a normal school for training army teachers was added in Turk's Row – the building now known as Cavalry House. Both of these are listed, the last as recently as 1998. In the second half of the nineteenth century the Asylum boys put on displays of gymnastics in the summer months on the surrounding lawns and these became a popular spectacle in late Victorian Chelsea. In 1901 a fine new gymnasium was built for them, now renamed Cadogan Hall. Later a running track was laid down round these lawns which became famous as the practice ground used by Roger Bannister and Christopher Chataway when they were training for the four minute mile.

Before 1870 local Parish schools, Church schools – both elementary and grammar – Chantry schools and Charity schools educated the poor. From 1824 bills calling for compulsory state education were repeatedly rejected by Parliament until the Compulsory Primary Education bill was finally passed in 1870. Dr Patricia Lin, in her unpublished doctoral thesis *Extending Her Arms*, has shown that the military schools, founded half a century earlier, were the real beginning of state education. The Royal Military Asylum was Britain's first co-educational, state-funded, state-administered school. Dr Lin argues that the reason Parliament was prepared to finance the military schools was the urgent need to encourage recruitment during the Napoleonic Wars. While France and Prussia maintained large standing armies by conscription the English Parliament, unable to forget James II's attempt to use the army against it, remained stubbornly opposed to conscription.

The education at the Asylum was based on the contemporary regime at Christ's Hospital. It consisted of reading, writing and simple arithmetic interspersed with lessons in trade and crafts; soon physical training was added. The sexes were segregated with the boys in the south wing and the girls in the north. In 1816 many of the girls were transferred to Southampton where a school had been opened for them. In 1827 the rest followed. A report in the School Chronicle of 1899 referred to the 1827 exodus as being necessary 'owing to the naughty, not to say giddy conduct of the fair sex, who were exiled to Southampton to the apparent and subsequent peace of the authorities at Chelsea'.

Teaching took place in one of the four great rooms leading off the main entrance hall. These rose to the height of two storeys with the windows of the second storey forming a clerestory. The boys were divided into classes each of which sat in a circle round its own instructor with the headmaster taking the best place nearest the fire. Work was set and during the class the boys came up individually to be tested on it. This was the tradition in the grammar schools from the 15th century, when great halls were built to accommodate between two and three hundred children, and it continued to be the norm in charity schools throughout the first half of the 19th century. The Asylum had a library and in 1808 £20 was spent on books for the boys. Equipment for games was provided, together with toys and musical instruments for the band; clowns and entertainers were regularly brought in and expeditions made to the Isle of Wight where the boys could enjoy the health-giving properties of sea bathing. On the other hand discipline was rigorous and punishment harsh, as it was at its model, Christ's Hospital.

Children were admitted from the age of 5 to 14 when they were discharged either to trade or the army, a choice they had to make by the time they were 12. Dr Lin found that, between 1803 & 1812, 43% of the boys went into trade, 29% into the army, 16% were withdrawn by parents, 6% were illegally detained by parents and 5% died.

The number of masters and ushers was very limited in most grammar schools and often there was only one master and an usher. This continued in the 18th century and into the 19th when even the sententious Dr Arnold at Rugby, a school which catered for children of the well-to-do, was making a virtue of necessity by running the school through the unruly older boys whose tyranny he licensed in exchange for some semblance of order in the rest of the school. At the Asylum, which did not have to rely on the uncertainties of voluntary contributions, there were still comparatively few teachers and so the Reverend Dr Andrew Bell's monitor system was introduced. This scheme was developed in Madras in 1795 whereby older and brighter boys were used to teach the younger ones. So successful was this that army schools in England and army outposts all over the world asked for monitors to come and give them short courses in the method. Then in 1812 training courses for sergeant-school-masters were started at the Asylum. They came from nearly every regiment in the country and within two years nearly 130 had been through the course. By 1812 the government was educating over 14,000 boys and girls in military schools at a cost of more than £81,000 a year.

The cult of athleticism in the public schools began at the beginning of the 19th century. It was started by the boys who organised games of football and cricket and was later taken up by their masters who decided that team games provided unrivalled training in leadership for officers and gentlemen. By contrast physical training, athletics and gymnastics, which were ignored in most public schools until the end of the 19th century, were introduced in the Asylum in 1823. The ideas were brought from Germany by P.H. Clias, the author of *An Elementary Course of Gymnastic Exercises* in which he describes walking, jumping, running and balancing exercises and a new style of swimming – the breaststroke.

After the Duke of York's death in 1827 the standards of education at the Asylum went into steep decline. By 1846 we find Henry Moseley, a school inspector, writing a confidential report for the Privy Council in which he stated that 'in the whole of my experience, now extensive in the inspection of secondary schools, I have visited none so little deserving of commendation'. By then the numbers of boys had fallen from a peak of 1,200, in 1823, to 330. The task of secular instruction was in the hands of six school-sergeants and a sergeant major of instruction. The inspector remarks: 'I have no other means of forming an opinion (of their qualifications) than that which is supplied me by the gross ignorance of the boys'. The school-sergeants 'carry canes and are permitted to use them for minor offences. Graver offences are punished by flogging, by confinement in a cage or a black hole, by carrying a log chained to the person or by the drill'. In one month there were 10 floggings of 12 stripes and 2 of 24 stripes and in the preceding month 17 of 12 stripes. The inspector found that 'as many floggings were inflicted on 350 boys at Chelsea in 6 weeks as upon 400 boys at Greenwich in a twelvemonth'. Twice as many boys were sick in the infirmary at Chelsea than at Greenwich and six had died the year before compared with one at Greenwich.

At Chelsea there was no apparatus for instruction – no blackboards, easels, maps or globes but they did have a lending library of 263 volumes. It does not seem to have been much used for the inspector goes on to criticise the boys' reading, spelling and arithmetic. 'In reading they make a measured pause after every word... In their manner of reading no reference whatever to the connection of the words is apparent or to the sense. No ray of intelligence lights up their faces as they read'. In his summary he expresses his 'sense of the injustice which has been done to these children in debarring them, almost from their infancy, from every element of instruction proper to the growth of their intellectual life'.

From The Graphic, *May 26th 1889*

Mr Moseley's report had its effect. A vote of censure was carried against the Commissioners, the Commandant, the Chaplain, the Doctor and everyone responsible for the management at Chelsea.

Reform quickly followed. The Asylum was remodelled and a new training school for regimental schoolmasters was set up, though initially with some resistance from the Horse Guards who expressed alarm at the idea of so much book-learning for prospective soldiers. But by 1850 the children, after learning 'the rudiments', were being taught the following subjects: Scripture; History of England, the Colonies, India, Greece, Rome and France; Arithmetic, slate & mental; Geography; Natural History; Grammar, Dictation & Composition; Object Lessons and Writing. More advanced boys went on to study Algebra, Mensuration and Fortification.

In 1856 there was a proposal to close the Asylum and turn it into a barracks; a protest meeting was called and a year or two later the idea was dropped. The Asylum continued as a military boarding school until 1909 when the boys were moved to new buildings in Dover where the school continues to flourish. The Asylum then became the London Headquarters of the Territorial Army until 1999 when it was sold back, after 200 years, to the original owner of the land, the Cadogan Estate, for commercial development and the laying out of the new Duke of York Square.

1999

Select bibliography

Cockerill, A.W., *Sons of the Free* (appendix A), Leo Cooper / Secker and Warburg, London, 1984; McIntosh, P.C., *Physical Education in England From 1800*, London 1952; Rudd, Lewis, *History of the Duke of York's Royal Military School 1801-1934*, Dover 1935; Seaborne, Malcolm, *The English School*, Vol. I, London, 1971

THE SCANDALOUS MEMBER FOR CHELSEA

Gerard Noel

Sir Charles Wentworth Dilke was born, and lived most of his life, at 76 Sloane Street, where he died in 1911. He represented the then new Parliamentary borough of Chelsea from 1868 to 1886. So successful, so famous and so popular was he as M.P. for Chelsea, that he was known, in his own lifetime, as well as to posterity, as "the Member for Chelsea".

Dilke had an unconventional upbringing in that ill-health prevented his going to school. But, by the age of 19, he was well enough not only to go up to Cambridge, which he did in the year 1862, but there, at Trinity Hall, to achieve the triple distinction of being senior legalist in the law tripos, President of the Cambridge Union and stroke of the boat which was head of the river in that year.

Cambridge was followed by an eventful trip around the world taking a whole year, during which he wrote long and numerous letters home. These letters became the basis of a remarkable book – a classic in its own way – published in 1866, entitled *Greater Britain*. In the words of Dilke's distinguished biographer, Roy Jenkins, the book gave him "not only considerable politico-literary reputation, but also a wide range of new contacts". The book was something of a "square circle", exhibiting Dilke as both an advanced radical and republican, and also a convinced imperialist. It was while working on this book that Dilke, now aged 24, was adopted as the Liberal candidate for Chelsea, a Parliamentary borough which, at this time, extended from just beyond his Sloane Street house on one side, as far as Hammersmith and Kensal Green on the other.

His climb to office was slow and, as Jenkins puts it, "laborious", partly due to internal rivalries within the Liberal Party, and partly due to the complicated political issues of the day. Having served as Under Secretary for foreign affairs from 1880 to 1882, he joined the Cabinet in the year 1882, as President of the Local Government Board, which at that time, was an important portfolio relating largely to Parliamentary reform. Dilke's great achievement at this period – and it took a considerable amount of skill, Parliamentary expertise, sheer determination and powers of persuasion – was to pilot through the House of Commons a bill for the redistribution of Parliamentary seats along more democratic – or, at least, less undemocratic – lines.

He was, in fact, at the peak of his powers, both mentally and physically, when, on the evening of July 18th., 1865, he returned home in high spirits from the Reform Club. A banquet had been held in his honour, to congratulate him in the piece of legislation just mentioned, the Redistribution Bill. Cheers were still ringing in his ears as he arrived at his house in Sloane Street, only to find, awaiting him there, a note from a certain Mrs. Rogerson, a close friend, or someone whom he then thought to be a close friend, asking him to call on her on the following morning as she had some grave information to give him. He went early on the next morning and learned that a certain Mrs. Donald Crawford, the young sister of his brother's widow, had confessed to her husband that soon after her marriage, Dilke had become her lover; and that Crawford in consequence, was proposing to sue for divorce and to name Dilke as co-respondent.

It was a shattering blow for Dilke. It was thought probable, at this time, that the ageing Prime Minister, Mr. Gladstone, might soon relinquish the leadership of the Liberal Party. Dilke was the obvious "heir apparent". Now all his dreams seemed to have been shattered.

Virginia Crawford, a kinswoman, as already noted, was 22 at the time. It was known, but not subsequently thought to be of crucial importance, that Dilke, many years earlier, had enjoyed a romantic dalliance with Mrs. Crawford's mother, Mrs. Eustace Smith. It is sometimes – but almost certainly, wrongly – supposed that this earlier liaison on Dilke's part may have, to some extent, motivated Mrs. Crawford in her accusations. It must be admitted, moreover that Dilke was known to have had casual affairs with several ladies. Again, almost certainly, however, Mrs. Crawford was not one of them. She, more than twenty years Dilke's junior, was not unattractive but certainly no great beauty. She was a frustrated woman at this point in her life. She was unhappy at home and at the age of 18, four years before making her accusations, she had married a dour Scottish MP in order to get away. She was never happy with him, never loved him and began to be unfaithful to him (though not with Dilke) within about a year of her marriage. Her lover was a certain Captain Henry Forster, whom Mrs. Crawford wanted to shield and with whom she was, without much doubt, in love; soon after the subsequent divorce case, however, Forster died.

Crawford was strikingly portrayed in a play called *Right Honourable Gentleman*, based loosely on Jenkins's book, as a dour and stern Victorian husband summoning his young wife into his room brandishing an insinuating anonymous letter and asking her, using a curious old fashioned expression, "Virginia, have you defiled my bed?" He then went on to say, "I have long suspected Forster." Mrs. Crawford, possibly panicking, hotly denied that Forster was her lover and then blurted out the expression "the man who ruined me was Charles Dilke". Gaining confidence, she added some further and sensational revelation, going as far as to say that Dilke "taught me every French vice".

What happened as the immediate result of this bombshell was that Crawford brought an action for divorce against Dilke, heard early in the following year, 1886. It was in every way an extraordinary case, one of the strangest ever to be brought, at least in the early days of the old Probate Divorce and Admiralty Division of the High Court.

The case for Crawford consisted almost entirely of a recitation, by Crawford, of his wife's confession which was uncorroborated except for the testimony, which was faulty and inconclusive, of two almost valueless witnesses. Nevertheless, the picture looked black for Dilke despite the fact, and this of course is extremely significant, that the judge, in his summing up said, "I cannot see any case whatever against Sir Charles Dilke".

Dilke, indeed, was discharged from the case, having been found in law to be an innocent man. Unfortunately, however, the situation was more complicated and, indeed, more tragic than this. Crawford's petition was granted on the grounds of his wife's adultery with Dilke. Now this verdict, strictly speaking, was correct in law but in practice, it meant that while Mrs. Crawford was found guilty of adultery with Dilke, Dilke was found not guilty of adultery with Mrs. Crawford. What on earth were the public at large to make of such an extraordinary verdict? Naturally, people were interested only in headlines, the sort of headlines which now proclaimed, "Charles Dilke named in sensational divorce case". So unsatisfactory, indeed, was this hearing for divorce, brought by Crawford against Dilke, that the Queen's Proctor was prevailed upon to intervene and to show cause why the decree given at this point should not be made absolute.

Dilke, however, was very badly advised by his counsel, Sir Charles Russell, one of the leading advocates of the day but not, it appears, fully conversant with the procedure of matrimonial law, which admittedly at this time was only in its infancy. Matrimonial law, in those days was catering for very few cases and was to undergo many changes before it became much more sophisticated years later. Be that as it may, Dilke not only found to his consternation, and contrary to the advice given him, that he would not be allowed to appear as a party in the case brought by the Queen's Proctor, but also he discovered that he would not be supported in court by Sir Charles Russell as he had hoped. He had confidently expected that Mrs. Crawford, on the supposition that she would also be a party to the case, would be subjected to what could only be a rigorous cross-examination by Sir Charles Russell. And it was thus confidently, indeed realistically, hoped by him that Mrs. Crawford's evidence would be totally destroyed.

As it was, the Queen's Proctor, no great friend of Dilke at the best of times, was represented in court by a certain Sir Walter Phillimore Q.C., who although a competent barrister, was by no means as formidable an advocate as his adversary in court, the man who was briefed by Crawford, namely Sir Henry Matthews Q.C., a high Tory and avowed enemy of Charles Dilke. Dilke appeared, as did Mrs. Crawford, as a witness only and was duly subjected to a withering cross-examination at the hands of Matthews. The worst part of all was that Dilke proved to be an extremely bad witness in his own defence. Even if, as we can legitimately suppose, he was telling the truth, his answers were so full of circumlocution and were so evasive as to put him apparently completely in the wrong.

Mrs. Crawford, on the other hand, had, by this time, become the hero of the hour, while Dilke was cast in the role of heavy villain. The jury took very little time to return a verdict which was unfavourable to Dilke who, only now felt certain that his career was finally ruined.

By this time it was the summer of 1886. Dilke was persuaded to stand again for Chelsea at the next election and was only narrowly beaten. From now on, he determined to try and clear his name by all legitimate means possible. He briefed a solicitor, who, with the help of agents, set out to track down all possible new evidence that might rehabilitate his good name. The evidence that came to light was little less than completely damning of Mrs. Crawford, who, it appeared, was far from being an innocent young woman, seduced by Dilke. Rather did it become apparent that she had several lovers and that she had unquestionably lied in the witness box.

One of her original allegations against Dilke, moreover, had been that, on one occasion, he had introduced a second lady into the bedroom, namely a young woman called Fanny Gray, an indoor servant whom Dilke persuaded to join himself and Mrs. Crawford in bed. This three-in-a-bed story was naturally very shocking to the public at large, but it was also said, in sophisticated social and political circles, that Mrs. Crawford could hardly have made up this story if it had not actually happened. This, however, is where the new evidence becomes very important. It was subsequently discovered, beyond any doubt, that Mrs. Crawford had made love to her principal paramour, Henry Forster, in the company of her own sister, Mrs. Harrison. In other words, this is almost certainly where the three-in-a-bed story came from. This is only one example of how the case, that had at one time seemed so formidable against Dilke, suddenly began to crumble and almost to disintegrate.

Unfortunately, however, all this came to light too late to be of any real service to Dilke even though a committee had been formed of respectable and influential men, some of them in public life, and by no means all of them special friends of Dilke. There was little, in practice, that they could do.

It was at this stage that an even more mysterious element enters into the whole conundrum. Whereas Dilke never ceased all his life to seek opportunities for clearing his name, Mrs. Crawford, shortly after the second case, seemed able to put the case entirely out of her mind and never referred to it again. Indeed the life of Mrs.

Sir Charles Wentworth Dilke

Crawford from that moment on was as different as can possibly be imagined to what her life had been before. It might be wrong to call her, up to then, a "loose woman" but she was by no means the innocent young damsel seduced by Dilke's charms that she would have wished to present herself to the world in the year 1886.

What happened was amazing and dramatic. She was a friend, as was Dilke in a different context, of the Cardinal Archbishop of Westminster of the day, Cardinal Henry Manning.

She told him of her desire to be received into the Roman Catholic Church. He explained the implications of this desire, and after her protestations that she was quite sincere, which he accepted, she eventually went to confession to Cardinal Manning, presumably admitting any misdeeds of her former life and, on receiving absolution, then received her first Holy Communion as a member of the Roman Catholic Church.

This circumstance adds another serious dimension into the whole situation. Did she confess all her "sins" to Manning? Or had she by now so successfully transferred events and occurrences, which had actually happened with Forster, over to Dilke? If so, did she confess this? Did she in fact confess that she had lied in the witness box and had seriously defamed the Member for Chelsea?

Well, of course, we will never know the answers to these questions. So sacrosanct is the "seal of confession" that Manning could never tell anyone what she said. But if she *had* confessed to telling monstrous lies about Dilke, he would have been bound to tell her that she could not receive absolution until she had made full "restitution" to Dilke and ensured the restoration of his good name. This would have involved her making some sort of public affirmation of Dilke's innocence and acknowledgement of her own mendacious accusations against him. But such a thing never happened. We are left then at the end of it all, with more of a mystery than ever.

Mrs. Crawford, born in 1865, did not die until she was over 80. More than half of her life was spent as a devout Roman Catholic, passionately involved in the social and charitable activities of her Church. She never remarried. She never again referred to Dilke. It was as if she had put all those parts of her life in a back room, locked the door, and never thought of them again. Was this a sure sign of her innocence or is there some much more intricate psychological explanation of this apparent metamorphosis of her life, possible showing some sort of almost schizophrenic ability to live at two levels? Perhaps indeed she had two totally different sides to her nature, one of which was in command of the first half of her life, and the other in command of the second. Mrs. Crawford seemed to live happily ever afterwards. Whether or not she ever thought about the misery which she had inflicted on Dilke and the total destruction she had wrought to both his private and public life, we shall never know.

1993

BRAM STOKER 1847–1912

Jane Dorrell

Born in Dublin in 1847 Bram Stoker was a sickly child (though he grew to be a stalwart 6ft. 2in.) who reputedly didn't leave his bedroom until he was 8 years old. He graduated with honours in science from Trinity in 1870 though he did not take his law finals until many years later. He was always stage-struck and seeing Henry Irving when he played in Dublin changed the course of his life. They became friends and when Irving invited him to be his business manager at the Lyceum he came to England with his beautiful wife Florence – who had once been courted by Oscar Wilde. They took a house in Cheyne Walk, number 27.

Stoker proved to be an egregious example of the Victorian work ethic. Between 1879 and 1906 he ran the Lyceum, organised Irving's American tours and accompanied him on his British ones; he was called to the bar – although he never practised – and he wrote eighteen novels, the most famous of which, 'Dracula', was published in 1897. He even found time to attempt to rescue a man who jumped into the Thames opposite his house. Although unsuccessful he was awarded the Royal Humane Society's Bronze medal.

'Dracula', in whom he brilliantly personified the age-old superstition of vampirism had been a success (though the bloodsucking Count did not become the household name he is today until after the 1931 film with Bela Lugosi) but in 1896 things began to go wrong. Irving was injured and was unable to act for some months and there was further disaster in 1898 when all the Lyceum's scenery and props were destroyed in a fire. Irving died in 1905 and with him, Stoker's salary. In 1906 he suffered a stroke which left him almost blind and it was then that he moved to a smaller house in St Leonard's Terrace. There, indefatigable to the end, he wrote his two-volume 'Personal Reminiscences of Henry Irving', an important contribution to the history of the English theatre. He died in 1912 – of exhaustion, the death certificate said.

1996

Two Chelsea Philosophers

Bob Barker

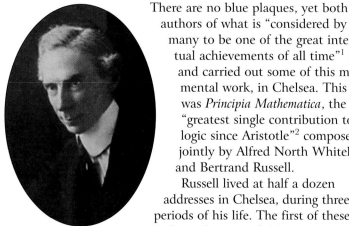

Bertrand Russell

There are no blue plaques, yet both authors of what is "considered by many to be one of the great intellectual achievements of all time"[1] lived, and carried out some of this monumental work, in Chelsea. This work was *Principia Mathematica*, the "greatest single contribution to logic since Aristotle"[2] composed jointly by Alfred North Whitehead and Bertrand Russell.

Russell lived at half a dozen addresses in Chelsea, during three main periods of his life. The first of these was in the early years of this century, towards the end of his first marriage; the second was in the Twenties, at the start of his second; and the third was in the Sixties, during his fourth. He had first rented 14 Cheyne Walk in the autumn of 1902 for six months, when he was aged thirty, and not yet famous, though he was putting the final touches to the work which was to make his name: *The Principles of Mathematics*. This explained how mathematics could ultimately be derived from logic, specifically from set theory, and answered the philosophical riddle of what numbers actually are. Russell had struggled for some years to state his new ideas in a consistent and systematic fashion, but was not fully satisfied with the result, and so had already begun collaborating with his former tutor, Whitehead, on the much more comprehensive and rigorous treatment which eventually became *Principia Mathematica*.

He was unsatisfied at this period for personal as well as for philosophical reasons. He had realised (suddenly, during an afternoon bicycle ride near Cambridge early in February 1902) that he no longer loved his wife Alys, but had not yet worked out a solution to that problem. To complicate matters, not only had he fallen out of love with Alys, but he now felt a strong, if probably Platonic, affection for Whitehead's wife, Evelyn, which had to be concealed from their respective spouses.

The riverside location of Cheyne Walk, however, did provide some consolation. His contemporary letters include such lucid passages as: "This place is singularly beautiful. Alone at night in my study at the top of the house, I see far below me the busy world hurrying east and west, and I feel infinitely remote from their little hopes and fears. But beyond, borne on the flowing tide of the river, the seagulls echo their melancholy cry, full of the infinite sadness of the sea; above, Orion and the Pleiades shine undisturbed." However, to his friend Gilbert Murray, he confided: "I feel horribly lost here. Only the river and the gulls are my friends."

Over the next decade or so Russell, with or without Alys, rented or stayed with friends at various other addresses in Chelsea and the mansion flats around Battersea Park. For example, in the autumn of 1903 and the spring of 1904, he returned to Cheyne Walk, first at number 13, and then back at number 14; the loveless home was described as "cheerless" and "uncared for" at the time. In the spring of 1905, Russell rented 4 Ralston Street and could write "I have learnt a *modus vivend*i with Alys...." This meant living, but not sleeping, together; neither of them was happy, and much of Russell's energy was now sublimated into what he described as "the absolute unbridled Titanic passion" of his work on the *Principia*.

While living in Ralston Street he dined out, for example, at Sidney and Beatrice Webb's, with such interesting fellow-guests as the actor Granville-Barker, then working as director at the (Royal) Court Theatre, and the current prime minister Arthur Balfour (himself formerly a philosopher and fellow member of Trinity College, Cambridge). By day Russell, in Edwardian moustache and high-necked collar, often enjoyed a constitutional walk around Battersea Park.

T.S. Eliot (later a graduate philosophy student of Russell's and another resident of riverside Chelsea) captured the paradoxical character and social impact of the young Russell famously in Mr *Apollinax*:

> his dry and passionate talk devoured the afternoon.
> 'He is a charming man' – 'But after all what did he mean?'

[1] Peter Hare: *Oxford Companion to Philosophy*
[2] *Concise Dictionary of National Biography*

Whitehead's character was somewhat less paradoxical; in Russell's words, he was "very modest", "kindly, rational and imperturbable... calm, reasonable and judicious", with a "profound and passionate devotion to wife and children" and had "delightful humour and great gentleness". He was, however, something of an absent-minded professor, especially where money and correspondence were concerned. He once said to Russell:

"You think the world is what it looks like in fine weather at noon day; I think it is what it seems like in the early morning when one first wakes up from deep sleep".

Until Volume I of *Principia Mathematica* was finally published, Russell was living largely on his private income, while Whitehead had for more than twenty years held a lectureship at Trinity College, Cambridge; however, in 1910, he relinquished this and helped to have Russell appointed virtually as his successor. By the spring of 1911, Whitehead was living in Chelsea, at 17 Carlyle Square; first lecturing at University College, and then becoming Professor of Applied Mathematics at Imperial College, Kensington in 1914-24.

Upon the completion of the *Principia*, Russell found that: "the long restraint gave way like the bursting of a dam. I found myself overwhelmingly and passionately in love." The sometimes slightly reluctant object of this new passion was Lady Ottoline Morrell, and the Whiteheads, who were not particularly fond of Alys, helped to foster the relationship. Russell asked Ottoline to go and talk things over with Evelyn in Carlyle Square; she subsequently described the experience as: "sitting in a strange elaborate little dining room, talking to a strange elaborate lady, who looked at me with suppressed mistrust and jealousy". At the end of March Russell stayed at the house, from which he wrote Ottoline several passionate letters, and where, on the morning of the 30th (in Ottoline's words):

"I had another interview with Bertie at the Whiteheads' house, to say goodbye, and to tell him that it was impossible for me to leave Philip, but he begged me to see him again. His despair weighed on me, and filled me with gloom. I felt it was impossible to cast him off."

And Russell wrote to her later that day:

"I still feel your arms around me and your kiss on my lips."

The following month, he was staying at the riverside flat of Gilbert Murray at More's Garden, Cheyne Walk, and wrote to Ottoline that Mrs Whitehead said: "we could meet occasionally at Carlyle Square, but not often, because she doesn't want her servants to know, or her son." Although he wrote Ottoline further passionate letters from Carlyle Square in May, and stayed there again in 1913, they did not again use the address as a meeting place.

Volumes II and III of *Principia Mathematica* were finally published in 1912 and 1913. Whitehead alone worked on a fourth volume, dealing with geometry, but never completed it. By 1917 he had moved to 12 Elm Park Gardens, and had parted company both philosophically and on the subject of the War with Russell, who spent the summer of 1918 in Brixton jail for publishing impolitic views about the latter. When he was released, Osbert Sitwell (then living at 5 Swan Walk) "organised a party for him the same evening, when Lady Ottoline Morrell took him to hear.... Bach and Mozart".

Whitehead meanwhile turned philosophically to more metaphysical questions which owed something to Bergson, for example analysing events in terms of process. This resulted in two quite important books: *An Enquiry Concerning the Principles of Natural Knowledge* (1919) and *The Concept of Nature* (1920). In 1920-21 he was back in Carlyle Square, although now a few doors down, at No.14. We can only wonder what this fundamentally quite conventional man made of the goings-on at no.2, where at the end of 1921 rehearsals were taking place for Edith Sitwell's radical *Façade*, with jazzy music by William Walton. A competing and contrasting noise was made by the local organ grinder, whom Sacheverell Sitwell vividly recalled playing *When Irish Eyes are Smiling* on the pavement outside in 1920 or 1921. Whitehead emigrated to the U.S.A (taking up a professorship at Harvard) in 1924.

Russell had married his second wife, Dora Black, at Chelsea Registry Office on 27 September 1921, six days after his divorce from Alys. By early November they were living at 31 Sydney Street, and on 16 November, in a room on the top floor, their son John was born. A few weeks later Countess Elizabeth von Arnim (third wife of Russell's brother Frank) wrote: "I've seen Bertie several times and his round little wife and their snug and happy little house in Chelsea, full of tiny jackets and pilchers and powder-puffs and cradles, with Bertie looking *perfectly* blissful." Russell was now almost fifty, and famous, or perhaps infamous. Hence he had had to take the then unusual step of buying the freehold; he could not rent as "I was politically and morally undesirable". Some of the furniture had been brought back by Bertrand and Dora from their stay in China; some of it he had acquired from Wittgenstein.

In 1922 and 1923, Russell stood as the Chelsea Labour parliamentary candidate. George Bernard Shaw considered this a hopeless cause, and wrote: "I suppose it is too late to urge you not to waste any of your own money on Chelsea, where no Progressive has a dog's chance. In Dilke's day it was Radical; but Lord Cadogan rebuilt it fashionably and drove all the Radicals across the bridges to Battersea." ("Dilke's day" would be when he was the Radical MP for Chelsea in 1868-86.) Russell was duly defeated by 8, 924 votes in the first election, and by 5,414 in the second. The house was often used as Labour Party Committee Rooms and a *Times* reporter wrote that: "a select body of workers toil zealously in the basement.... the surroundings are pleasantly marked by the owner's good taste." However, a tomato was once thrown through the window, perhaps by a disgruntled Conservative. Meanwhile Alys, who never entirely ceased to love Russell, was living nearby at St. Leonard's Terrace and poignantly "caught glimpses of him at lectures or concerts occasionally, and through the uncurtained windows of his Chelsea house, where I used to watch him sometimes reading to his children."

Russell turned increasingly to writing as a career and on the whole he did his popular, money-making, writing at Sydney Street in the winter, and his more technical work in Cornwall in the summer. Hence the 'lighter' works mostly written in Sydney Street are: *Prospects of Industrial Civilisation* (with Dora, 1923) which was not a great success; a pair of shorter and, in their day, more successful books: *The ABC of Atoms* (1923) and *The ABC of Relativity* (1925); and *What I Believe* (1925).

Alfred Whitehead

After the Second World War, Russell succeeded to the family earldom and became for a time almost a member of the Establishment; he gave the first Reith lectures in 1948, and received the Nobel prize for literature in 1950. Alys continued to live in Chelsea (latterly in Wellington Square) and towards the end of her life, in 1949-50, she and Bertrand were able to meet again on friendly terms. She arranged his 78th birthday party, on 18th May 1950, at which, she said, he talked brilliantly for four hours. Although, after this, he lived mostly in North Wales, Russell and Edith, his fourth wife, kept a Chelsea *pied à terre* at 43 Hasker Street from about 1960 to 1965. Here were a "study full of worn academic books and row upon row of detective stories in glass fronted cases". Even now, Russell did not shun controversy, and in his autobiography he describes returning there in September, 1961, after his second brief term in Brixton gaol (forty-three years after his first, and the result this time of his anti-nuclear activities): "We delighted in our reunion in freedom very early on Monday morning. But almost at once were besieged by the press and radio and TV people who swarmed into Hasker Street."

He was eighty-nine at the time.

1997

CHELSEA HOUSEBOATS

The Boat People

Lewis Kennedy

Peter Osgood looks fondly at a familiar Chelsea view and remarks, "Really, it is an offshore village." He is talking about the fifty-eight houseboats lying in the Thames above Battersea Bridge at moorings administered by the Chelsea Yacht and Boat Co., which he runs and which celebrates its 60th anniversary in 1995.

It is older than that, of course. The eastern stretch of the moorings is on the site of the Greaves family's boatyard, from which Charles Greaves would row Turner across the river to Battersea to paint sunsets and where his sons, the artists Walter and Henry Greaves, worked and took Whistler on the Thames for the inspiration that produced his "nocturnes". The western end was a wharf where sailing barges discharged coal; the two-storey building still standing on the wharf was then stables for the horses that pulled the coal carts.

Then in 1935, the Chelsea Yacht and Boat Co. was founded by Charles Fleming, a handsome, dashing young businessman, who ran it with style until his sadly premature death a quarter of a century later; Osgood's office-boat bears his name. At first the business was mainly building and repairing river craft. One elderly man, who worked there in those days, remembers the cold-storage lighters that were repaired, or rebuilt, there, before being towed downstream to the docks where they would be loaded with frozen meat from New Zealand. There was a recreational side of it, too, and several Chelsea families kept sailing dinghies on the moorings for weekend expeditions on the river. During the war, the company built naval launches and water-carrier barges, the yard and its boat-building workshop in Lots Road employing some eighty workers. The houseboats did not arrive until the idea was prompted by the post-war housing shortage.

At first, they were mostly assault landing-craft, some of which had seen action on D-Day, motor torpedo-boats, motor launches and pinnaces, which were converted by the yard's shipwrights. Over the years, as they gradually became more decrepit, they were encased in steel outer hulls and a few still are. The most famous of all, and is, the former MTB 219, which, commanded by the late, much-decorated Mark Arnold-Forster, took part in the near-suicidal daylight attack on the German battleships *Scharnhorst* and *Gneisnau*, as they made their famous dash up the Channel in 1942; she is still on her moorings.

Charles Fleming also built a mock-up of a Mississippi stern-wheeler on piles off Battersea Park for the 1951 Festival of Britain pleasure gardens, and pleasure-boats with dragon figureheads for the lake at Longleat. When he died, Peter Osgood's father took over the firm and was himself succeeded by his son nearly twenty years ago.

"Now the business is mainly managing and maintaining moorings and the houseboats but we still build and repair boats ourselves," he said. The houseboats themselves are in two stretches of moorings with a gap between them; which had been the old barge-breaking beach and which was kept open on the insistence of a resident of Cheyne Walk, who complained that the houseboats would obscure her view of the river.

The houseboats are privately owned and change hands for between £38,000 and £250,000. The annual mooring fees are currently £55 per foot of the craft's overall length and the maintenance fees (including the newly-installed vacuum drainage linked with the London sewer system, access lighting, mail delivery and the services of a night watchman) are £23 per foot. Boat-owners pay their own insurance, water, electricity and telephone bills, of course.

The houseboats have faced three major threats. The first two were from proposed trunk roads that would slice across this bend in the river, to which the Embankment was never extended. The management had to prepare four relocation schemes but, so far, all plans for such a road have been shelved and the boats continue to ride where they have for so long. Since the last threat evaporated, the moorings have been upgraded with steel piling and pontoons linking the houseboats, instead of the rickety boat-to-boat gangways of the former picturesque jumble, and the new drainage system. The other threat was, surprisingly, from the river-buses, which, to the regret of so many Chelsea people, stopped running in 1993, when the Government refused to provide a temporary subsidy. Osgood explains, "You may have noticed that the riverbuses slowed down as they passed our moorings and assumed that their wash caused us

The Boat Yard from Battersea Bridge

no trouble. That was not the case because their waterjets churned up the river so that it never really calmed. The river-bed was washed away to such an extent that ancient piles and stakes, which had been buried in the mud for a century or more, emerged from it and the beach itself was eroded."

Peter Osgood is amused by the belief that the houseboat people are the last of the wild Chelsea bohemians. "We are a very normal Chelsea community, " he maintains. "We have civil servants, actors, a cleaner, artists, business people, musicians, all sorts living here. In the past we have had a few celebrities – the actress Dorothy Tutin amongst them – and plenty of famous visitors, including Douglas Bader, Peter Sellers and Laurence Olivier. Oddly, if you mention the houseboats in almost any London gathering, nine times out of ten someone will say that they know somebody who had lived here. There is one little mystery: for some unknown reason, more women than men seem to choose to live afloat."

1994

CHELSEA AT WAR

Before

Tom Pocock

It was a sunny September afternoon in 1933 and I was leaning out of an upstairs window of a corner house in Oakley Crescent, which is now called Oakley Gardens. Across the street, at least half the houses were shabby, with old lace curtains, for Chelsea people were then far more of a social and economic mixture than they are now. Looking down through the leaves of the lime trees in our garden, I could see that there were no cars about, except our own, parked briefly outside the gate before being "put away" at Tankard and Smith's garage in the King's Road, where Waitrose now trades.

Perhaps the lavender-seller was standing in the road, like an Augustus John model in a long gipsy dress, a basket of lavender on her arm, singing "Buy my sweet lavender" in a fine contralto voice. Or the muffin man might have been striding by, ringing his bell, with a wooden tray of muffins and crumpets, covered with green baize, balanced on his head. Or the Walls ice cream man on his tricycle, ringing his bell and calling out "Walls ices – they're lovely!".

What I know for certain is that, as I looked from the window, I heard a distant drone, which grew louder until I saw, above the chimney-pots of Oakley Street a formation of silver aeroplanes. As an eight-year-old, I immediately recognised them as Hawker Hart biplane bombers of the Royal Air Force. Then another formation of small biplanes approached from the direction of Kensington and I recognised these as Hawker Fury fighters. As the two formations drew together, a red flare was fired from the cockpit of the leading fighter and the two squadrons veered apart. Later my father read a newspaper report to me announcing that in the annual exercise of the defences of London, approaching bombers had been successfully intercepted and driven off by defending fighters.

There was another such exercise five years later but it was very different because it was held at night. We had been told that bombers would be over London and I lay awake in the dark listening to their engines throbbing above. When I looked out of the window, all I could see was the red glare in the sky to the north from the electric sign on the front of the new Gaumont Cinema – which is Habitat today – and wondered whether real fires would look like that.

Neighbours were becoming involved in Air Raid Precautions, sometimes being given mysterious titles such as "Warden". One A.R.P. official called at our house to advise on this. I remember standing in the kitchen – a smaller version of the upstairs-downstairs kitchen – with its solid pine table, dresser, new-fangled refrigerator and large, wicker armchair, beneath the flattened cushion of which I knew the maid kept her twopenny romantic magazines. This, he was saying, is the best room to make gas-proof because all you will need is a wet blanket stretched across a wooden frame that can be fitted over the window. In the event my parents decided not to do this. If war came, they thought – although they did not tell me – London would be devastated by bombs and poison gas within a week, so "evacuation" would be best. My father might have to remain at Broadcasting House but the rest of us would go to stay with an uncle in the country.

As the spring of 1939 became summer, a sense of doom and resolution seemed to grow. I remember walking to Sloane Square one morning with my father – myself dressed for school; he in his professional uniform of black homburg hat, grey pin-striped suit and pigskin attaché case – and him telling me that he had been talking to "high-ups in the Government", who had been watching the latest RAF exercise. "They told me that the sky was black with our fighters", he said. Such was the British secret weapon: self-confidence.

Barrage balloons, sagging like great, grey elephants, appeared in Battersea Park and when aloft would form a surreal ceiling over London. Concrete and sandbag blast-walls appeared in front of the entrances to Government offices and police stations. There was bustle at the Town Hall, where our neighbours in A.R.P. would look important in their uniforms. Some of them were retired, or were living on modest independent incomes, and they acquired a new look of confidence and purpose. But what would happen we could only guess and imagine after seeing horrifying photographs of the civil war in Spain.

Before it began, we had gone to the country and did not return until the Blitz had ended a year and a half later. There were more dangers to come, of course, but during the first eighteen months of the war, Chelsea had, when seen from exile, an heroic quality. It seemed to be standing on the ramparts. It was.

CHELSEA AT WAR

During

———

Frances Faviell

Those first days of the *Luftwaffe's* Blitz on Chelsea were dramatic and tragic, and in them the much-resented and ridiculed air-raid wardens came into their own and showed us the stuff of which they were made. Our Chelsea ones were magnificent!

The first to rouse people after the sirens sounded, they hurried to the shelters, ticking off the names of the residents in their areas as they arrived, then back they went to hustle and chivvy the laggards and see that those who chose to stay in their homes were all right. The first to locate and report the bombs to Control, they were the ones to guide and direct the Services sent by Control to the "incident" (a word to which we were to become all too accustomed). It was the wardens who soothed and calmed the terrified and comforted the injured and the dying. They carried children, old people, bundles of blankets, and the odd personal possessions which some eccentrics insisted on taking with them to the shelters. They woke the heavy sleepers, laughed at the grumblers, praised the helpful and cheerful, and performed miracles in keeping law and order during those first dramatic weeks when the Battle of London was being fought in our skies.

One of the first horrors was a direct hit on Cadogan Shelter, a public shelter under a block of flats in Beaufort Street. The blast killed a large number of people as it blew in the sides of the shelter. Our first casualties at F.A.P.5 (*First Aid Post*) were quiet and shocked. None of them wanted to say much – I think the dirt and mess with which they were covered and their anxiety for missing relatives or friends was uppermost. The casualties' indifference to injuries, cuts, and abrasions astonished us just as the dirt upset all our arrangements. The effects of shock when they first arrived, although we had been trained to recognise them, varied very much in individual cases. What did emerge from this first tragedy was a feeling that shelters were not safe – that had the victims stayed at home they would still be alive. To this there was no answer – it was

After the raid: the search for survivors in Edith Grove, 1941

the duty of all Civil Defence personnel to encourage the public to use the shelters...

The Blitz was providing something besides bombs. It was making people talk to one another. People in shops, in the buses, in the streets often talked to me now. They opened up amazingly about how they thought and what they thought – how they felt and what they felt. They all liked to see the nurses' uniforms – and were loud in their praise of the nurses, the firemen, and the wardens. But they did not like the indignity of sleeping publicly in a bunk in a shelter with hundreds of others. The Blitz was doing something else – it was continuing the slow difficult process already begun before the war of breaking down class barriers.

Another shelter received a direct hit in our area on the 13th and very early in the morning we had many casualties at the F.A.P. This was the large shelter of Manor Buildings, an L.C.C. block of flats in Flood Street. The water main had been severed and the poor sufferers were soaking wet. We put them all with their feet in hot water and wrapped in blankets until they could be got dry things. They were all filthy and had a lot of cuts and bruises and were all suffering from shock. Shelters were rapidly getting a bad name and some of the casualties said that it was obvious that they could be seen from the air! Residents in Paultons Square had no gas at all as a bomb

had severed the gas main. It had also killed one of the wardens in the hut there.

The bomb and everyone's special bomb was still a subject of endless interest and possibilities – but they were coming so thick and fast that everyone had a better story than his neighbour. All over London people were full of stories of the Blitz, but life was going on as usual – in spite of it. September 14th was a date which few of the personnel at Post Don will forget. In a further day-light raid another shelter was hit – this time under a church. The Church of the Holy Redeemer is a massive building and I had been there several times to see the shelter in the crypt because some of our refugees liked the idea of this shelter so much that they wanted to change to it. It was very close to Cheyne Hospital and when, at first, two of them did go there, I had gone to see that they were all right; but we persuaded them that it was too far and that their own was just as safe. It was a very popular shelter – perhaps because, like the refugees, others felt that nowhere would be safer than under the protection of the Church – and at the time the bomb fell it was crowded.

The bomb was recorded by one of us telephonists in the Control Centre at 18.35. The message said that there was a fire and casualties trapped in Holy Redeemer Church in Upper Cheyne Row. Requests followed in rapid succession for ambulances, blankets to cover the dead, fire services, and reports came in that there were many casualties.

The bomb had struck the church at an angle through a window in a most extraordinary way and had penetrated the floor and burst among the shelterers, mostly women and small children. Here George Thorpe, whom we knew as 'Bert', lost his life with those women and children whom he had visited to reassure them – as he always did, although he was not the shelter warden. He knew that they were apt to become nervous and needed moral support in the heavy raids and he used to drop in there to boost up their courage and cheer them up.

The bomb exploded right amongst the shelterers. A woman who was in the shelter told me about it when I visited her afterwards in St. Luke's Hospital. She was badly injured and said that the scene resembled a massacre – in fact, she compared it to an engraving she had seen of the massacre of the women and children of Cawnpore in the Indian Mutiny, with bodies, limbs, blood, and flesh mingled with little hats, coats, and shoes and all the small necessities which people took to the shelters with them.

We often dined at the Café Royal and also at the Royal Court Hotel in Sloane Square. Mr. Wilde, the Manager, had been most kind and helpful. We sometimes remarked on the large amount of glass in the dining-room, the walls of which were almost covered with mirror-glass, giving the illusion of very great space. The hotel had a deep strongly reinforced air-raid shelter for its residents of which Mr. Wilde was justly proud. He himself was always in evidence on noisy evenings when the bombs were near, reassuring the guests.

On the night of November 12th we had dined there rather early and the sirens had sounded while we were having dinner. Richard had to go on fire-duty at the Ministry and I had left him at the entrance to Sloane Square Station and hurried home in case I was called. It was not my evening for duty but several nurses had colds and I had said that I would be available if needed. I had hardly reached home when a terrific thud shook the road, but I could see nothing. The wardens were out, and there was activity in the sky and the barrage was pretty heavy, but the great thud had not been located immediately.

About half past ten the telephone rang and someone called me to go at once to the Royal Court Hotel. The line was very bad, almost impossible to hear, and it was with difficulty that I had got the message at all. As I had only just left the hotel I presumed that I had left something valuable behind there. I rang the F.A.P. and said that I had just been called by someone to go to the hotel, and to my astonishment the V.A.D. who answered the telephone said, 'Yes, Mobile Unit has just gone there.'

The square presented an amazing sight – two great flaming jets guarded the pit which had once been the station. The bomb had severed the gas main, the firemen shouted to me as I tried to pick my way across to the Royal Court Hotel, and the newly built station had just disappeared into the depth below. They were already bringing out the first dead and injured and carrying those requiring immediate treatment into the hotel.

Mr. Wilde and the staff were splendid. Table napkins, towels, blankets, and rugs all appeared as we laid the injured down in the lounge and hall. It was a pretty grim business – and again the appalling dirt was the most striking thing. It was evident that getting the bodies out was going to take all that night and many more. The bomb had fallen as a train was leaving the station, and the rear carriage was caught directly – the remainder of the train was shot by the blast almost to South Kensington station. This incident was ghastly as regards the holocaust of human flesh. Identification was almost impossible – and bodies were put together roughly on stretchers and some of them taken into nearby houses to be pieced together later somehow. The worst casualties were the Underground staff who had been in the canteen on the station when the bomb fell. There were fourteen men, one conductress, and two attendants in the canteen. By the following Saturday – the bomb having fallen on the Tuesday previously – there had been thirty-eight stretchers of human flesh pieced together – but there were still seventeen people to be accounted for.

The smell of explosions was very pungent, and one that stuck in the nostrils afterwards. The dust and plaster smelt, too, an ancient timeless smell and in Sloane Square there had been a terrifying smell of gas. All round it buildings were damaged and the square strewn with wreckage and glass. Only the ultra-modern, newly designed Peter Jones building stood proudly without a pane of its acres of glass broken. This was explained by the caving in of the station itself so that the blast went up the Underground tunnel and the actual explosion was muffled. At first they did not realise that it was so near, and the cries of those below on the station were muffled too by debris which had descended on them from above...

On 16th April, 1941, another heavy raid began:
That it was our worst night yet was on everybody's lips – and when news came in that the Old Church had gone it seemed the climax to the mounting horrors. The Old Church – I thought of it on that Sunday of March 23rd with all those Sea and A.T.C. Cadets in it – with the daffodils coming out around More's and Hans Sloane's tombs. 'It's a pile of dust ' one of the stretcher-bearers said. 'The whole of that bit – all Petyt Place seems to have disappeared – and the fire-watchers with it.'

Soon after we digested this it was quiet – and at long last the welcome distant sirens sounded far away – then nearer – and then loudly our own from the Albert Bridge proclaimed that the raid was over.

The All Clear had sounded at five minutes to five; it had been one of the longest raids we had known – all but eight hours. In the cold pale morning light we surveyed the appalling havoc of what had been our small colony in the Royal Hospital Road. How we had ever emerged from the mess that had been our home seemed incredible – it was one huge pile of rubble, and more had fallen since we had left it... but close at hand a blackbird was singing gloriously.

Picking our way across the piles of glass was perilous, and when I saw in the mess something which looked like a garment and found it was a very old camel-hair coat of mine I fell upon it as if it were the most valuable mink. It was indescribably filthy – but it was a coat, an old friend, and as far as I could see we had no material possessions left in the world. My dress had been blasted off below the hips and I had only an overall – the coat was warm and the early morning air struck chill...

It was not easy to drive anywhere – the streets were blocked by great mounds of fallen masonry, glass and debris. All along the Embankment the firemen's hoses lay across the wide street and houses sprawled with the vitals and bones spread out. The Old Lombard Restaurant had been almost demolished and men were digging on it as we passed. The top stories of Cheyne Hospital appeared to have been badly damaged, but as we came to the Old Church we stopped appalled, and got out of the car. I had heard about the horror of the night there – but its reality surpassed imagination. One great mound of dust was all that was left of the lovely little church – and men were digging all over it! The sun shone on the gap where Petyt Place had been – removed as if with giant tongs. The vicar was safe – but the entire fire-watching party, including seventeen-year-old schoolboy Michael Hodge, home for the holidays, had all perished with the exception of one member.

Chelsea, April 19th 1941

All up Old Church Street there were smoking ruins and masses of glass and debris sprawled everywhere. A heavy acrid smell lingered in the air in spite of the breeze from the river – the smell we had come to identify with the Blitz.

There were many stories of the night of April 16th – already known as 'the Wednesday'. The German parachutist had actually landed almost on the church and had given himself up to the wardens, who were at first at a loss to know what to do with him. There had been parachute mines on Cheyne Walk, Cranmer Court, the Old Church, and our one on Cheyne Place, as well as the Royal Hospital Infirmary, Dovehouse Street, and Sutton Dwellings, and high-explosive bombs on the Elms Garage, Post E in Cale Street, Chelsea Square, and many off the Embankment, as well as hundreds of incendiaries. There had been a very large number of casualties and terrible damage. Several firemen had been killed and many wardens injured.

Chelsea's last heavy raid of the eight months' Blitz came on May 10/11th. There had been bad incidents on the Saturday following 'the Wednesday', but it was on May 11th, when the Houses of Parliament were hit, that Chelsea suffered most. The Red Cross and St. John's did magnificent work on both these occasions and were warmly praised, with the whole A.R.P. Services. On May 11th a heavy bomb fell through the operating theatre of St. Luke's

The ruins of Chelsea Old Church after the bombing

Hospital, killing two doctors and several nurses and wrecking two wards, the radiography and kitchen departments, and most of the reception halls as well as the doctors' quarters. The hospital had to be closed for the simple reason that it could no longer be run.

Thousands of incendiaries were showered on Chelsea during that raid and many high-explosive bombs fell in the river. Work was hampered by a blazing barge loaded with paper outside Phillips Mills and the air was thick with little pieces of black charred paper like a black snowstorm. The acrid smell of burning paper was quite overpowering and suffocating to the firemen and wardens fighting the blaze. The shower of charred paper like a flickering curtain silhouetted against the flames was an eerie and unforgettable spectacle.

The closing of St. Luke's Hospital, combined with the loss of more friends both in the R.A.F. and at sea, was for me another landmark in the war, but although we did not know it at the time, May 11th was to mark the end of the eight months' Blitz on London. Three years were to elapse before Chelsea's foundations were to be shaken by an 'incident' (February 23rd, 1944), the magnitude of which was to make all the preceding ones seem small.

1990

Extracts from Chelsea Concerto *by the late Frances Faviell, published by Cassell in 1959.*

CHELSEA AT WAR

The Wednesday

———

Theodora FitzGibbon & June Buchanan

Of all the disasters that befell Chelsea during the Second World War, the most memorable was the bombing of the Old Church. It was the heart and soul of the place and its destruction was, at first, met with disbelief. Its subsequent resurrection, together with most of its monuments and furnishings, was thus all the more inspiring.

Two new accounts of the events of the night of 16th-17th April, 1941 – the occasion that became known as "The Wednesday" – have just come to light. Both describe the experiences of girls living nearby. The first was written, forty years on, by Theodora FitzGibbon, widow of the writer Constantine FitzGibbon, in her memoir *With Love* (Century Publishing, £8.95); she was then an aspiring actress and artists' model, living with the painter Peter Rose Pulham in King's Mansions, Lawrence Street. The second, pencilled into a diary at the time and never published, is by our present Chelsea neighbour June Buchanan (née Spencer); she was then a very young ambulance driver lodging at 97 Cheyne Walk with other friends of the late Richard Stewart-Jones, an Hon. Secretary of the Chelsea Society, who was to become the prime mover in the rebuilding of Chelsea Old Church.

Theodora FitzGibbon wrote: –

There was a thud as if a gigantic sack of coal had been dropped, making the room shudder, almost immediately another thud, and a tremendous explosion. The window blew in and a dense cloud of greenish dust moved slowly through the gaping hole, forming into the shape of a weird monster. Peter flung himself on top of me on the bed, his eyes wide and dark with fear. His face and lips, pressed on to mine, tasted gritty.

'Dear Pussy, dear Pussy.'

There was a noise like exceptionally heavy rain, and his weight became almost unbearable. The bedside light was still on: the clock said twenty-five past one. All the furniture had moved, not far, it had all just moved round about a foot, except for the chair with my clothes on which had been under the window. There was no sign of that. I could move only my head, for the bed was covered with lumps of plaster, broken glass, wood and what looked like small stones. Peter's face was thickly covered with greenish-white dust, his eyes luminous, and large by contrast, like a clown's

'I'm all right, darling, I think. But what happened? There were those thuds, it didn't sound like a bomb.'

'Well, if it wasn't a bomb, I don't know what has brought the ceiling and walls down. You're right, though, it wasn't the usual long shriek.'

'Should we turn the light out?'

'In a minute, when I've got you free.'

'Find me a coat or something, all my clothes have disappeared. There's a torch under my pillow.'

Through the open window came the sound of excited voices. I turned my head to look out, and saw leaping flames quite nearby.

'I can see fires.'

'That's not unusual.'

'But it is. Normally all I can see is the church clock tower.'

He framed his face in his hands and peered out through the fog-like dust.

'I can't see the church either. I think it's gone. There are fires everywhere. I must get you out, Pussy.'

Dressed in a long orange chiffon nightdress, brown brogue shoes and my top-coat, I switched off the light and by torchlight we crept along the corridor. Peter picked up his overcoat from the bathroom floor, where it had been blown. It was like walking on a shingly beach. There was no front door, just a frame, and a pile of glass and wood.

'Cigarettes. Damn, look in the sitting room.'

From the first floor somebody shouted up:

'Come down slowly by the wall, the stairs may not be there.'

Peter went first and held my hand tightly. Ahead of us we heard footsteps on the stone staircase, which was littered with debris.

'Some of the banisters have gone. Go slowly, sit down if necessary, and come down that way.'

We sat down, slithering on our bottoms like children.

In the street were the occupants from the lower floors, wardens, ambulances, nurses, firemen and police, all lit by torchlight, the wardens with their log-sheets hanging round their necks. Someone tried to herd me into an ambulance but I pulled away, and Peter and I went into the Cross Keys, which was wide open, the door and one wall blown into the bar. The elderly couple who ran it, never known for their generosity, were sitting down sipping brandy, covered in white plaster, looking dazed and very, very old, amongst the people gathered there. A local resident was in charge and gave us all a drink.

'The Old Church has gone!'

This was repeated frequently: that they were alive seemed incomprehensible. We soon left, and went towards the remains of Chelsea Old Church to see if we could help. The nurses' home of the Cheyne Hospital for Children had the top floor blown off: a neat nurse's bedroom, the ceiling light still shining, looked like a stage set. A warden perilously climbed up the bombed staircase and switched it off, although there was a flaming gas main burning around the corner which floodlit the entire area. The church was nothing but an immense heap of timber and stone, flames licking through it; a large vaulted tomb with a stone urn on top rose up undamaged in the front. The New Café Lombard and all the large and small houses at the end of Old Church Street had been flung together into a giant mountain of shale-like destruction, all lit by the fires and the gas main. Under that fantastic mountain were people, some still alive. Heavy stones were flung aside like pebbles: the local grocer of the street, Mr Cremonesi, put his hand down through a space and felt warm flesh. A naked unhurt woman was pulled up. An old lady appeared, staggering, from the far side of the mountain, having been flung at least thirty yards and then covered with glass, wood and bricks, from which she had extricated herself. She seemed unhurt. A curious rattling sound like a time-bomb made us cautious: a battered tin was moving on a piece of stick. Below, the young woman had forced it through the bricks to attract attention. She was rescued by a war reserve policeman. A sixteen-year-old girl, pinned, only her head showing, talked to a rescue worker: she was freed, but died several hours later.

Young and old brought buckets of water to supply stirrup pumps to douse the fires. The dust was like a great fog. Charred papers and smouldering wood choked the helpers. Still the raid continued with whining bombs, cracking, thudding guns, droning aeroplanes, both German and our own night-fighters. Huge chandeliers of flares hanging in the sky like Roman candles illuminated the bomber's targets. Our hands were cut and bleeding, and when I saw the

Ruins of Chelsea Old Church, 1941

why the usual whining sound was absent. All the fire-watchers at my post had been killed except Arthur Mallett... One of the mines had landed beside him and the other fire-watchers.

'For Christ's sake, run!' he had cried.

He had run so fast he couldn't stop in time to turn the corner into Old Church Street with the others... He'd crouched behind a small iron post, seconds before the second mine landed, which also detonated the first one.

'Blimey, ' he said laconically, 'that lot's gone.' All he had lost was the trouser on his right leg. Now he wanted a cup of tea, and to find his sister, so over the mountain he went, and met her halfway in that pitiful no-man's-land.

The Thames was at low tide, factories in flames opposite, as we smoked our cigarettes leaning over the wall near the steps leading down to the river. Bombs were dropping all round, but we were too exhausted to bother. So long as we could see them, we said. Down on the silty river-bank a man was walking about.

'There's a man down there, Peter.'

'Probably a fireman looking for an unexploded bomb.'

'Well, he's coming towards the steps. Let's go down and see. It's cold standing here.'

It was light enough to walk easily down the steps, and we were about half-way down as he was coming up. Over Peter's shoulder, I said:

'Looks like air force uniform. Hope it's one of ours!'

'Don't be so imaginative, Pussy.'

As they met face to face I heard:

'*Leutnant-*' and some German numerals followed.

Peter stood aside, and the German airman stood on the steps between us.

'*Ich spreche Deutsch, *' I said.

He repeated only what he had said to Peter, and we walked up in silence to the top.

The airman looked about twenty-three, the same age as myself; his face was pale with terror. He did and said nothing, just stood with his arm at his side, as is understandable when someone has just parachuted into an area which he has been bombing. Wardens and firemen came round, in fact one fireman had a hose ready in case he attacked us. Nobody knew quite what to do with this man who had dropped from the sky. The airman suddenly lurched forward, as a man who none of us had seen kicked him hard in the backside. The man then rushed to the front and wrenched a pistol

blood on Peter's hands I felt suddenly sick and faint. He led me down to the Embankment. Although the day had been warm, a breeze came off the river and it was chill. He held me close to warm me. Several wardens, police and onlookers were there talking. Two land-mines had been parachuted down on the church, which was from a pocket on the pilot's flying suit. Peter, usually slow-moving, quickly stretched out his long arms and wrested it away. It all happened so quickly, in the dim light, that only those close by realized what was going on. Two war reserve policemen materialized from nowhere, and quite quietly they marched off the German airman between them. Someone said: 'Like a drunk and disorderly on a Saturday night' – except that the captive marched firmly and erectly, and there was no disorder.

Without speaking to each other, Peter and I followed at a distance. We had been shocked by the pistol episode; death on the ground was more real and immediate than from the skies; and despite all our horrors of the long night, we both knew that the young boy was frightened too. In a funny way, he was 'our parachutist' and we wanted to see him in safe keeping. What can he have been thinking as he walked through the ruined streets, fires blazing in all of them, bombs still raining down?

The policemen marched him into Chelsea Police Station, and we were just leaving when other policemen came out and spoke to us. We went in, and reported as accurately as we could. At about four o'clock in the morning, two more parachute mines exploded nearby – one in front of the police station, and the other behind, but the block of flats, Cranmer Court, took the brunt. They gave us a cup of strong sweet tea, which tasted like nectar. The orange chiffon nightdress was in flitters up to my knees from the rubble shifting. We borrowed a pair of scissors and cut it straight. Even so we must have looked a comical couple, still covered in dust, blood and dirt. A few minutes before five o'clock the 'all clear' went, after eight hours of continuous bombing. It was the second heaviest raid on London, and became known as 'the Wednesday'.

June Buchanan wrote:

97 Cheyne Walk, April 15th, 1941, Tuesday.
Free day shopping on my bicycle all day – back to tea – Film in evening with John D.

April 16th, 1941, Wednesday.
On duty 8-4pm. Very warm spring day. The square gardens are a mass of flowers. In the evening out to dine with Sydney Cuthbert (on leave, Scots Guards). We dine at the Spanish restaurant, Soho, in the ARP-wine cellar. Heavy bombing shaking everything by 9.30.

Came out to find Piccadilly blazing – to The 400 [*the night-club in Leicester Square*] to dance for 2 hours – bad news of Chelsea.

Impossible to find a taxi-driver, so we walked (I was wearing a long pink and black tulle dress!). Fires were raging all around – very heavy bombing. We threw ourselves to the pavement a few times. Got a lift from Cadogan Square. Incendiary bombs all down the King's Road.

Got to the ambulance station (opposite the Old Church). It was quite flat, and most of Cheyne Walk, too. Glass in windows puffed out as you looked at them. I hunted for ambulance people and found all were safe (they had all been called out to the Royal Hospital just before).

One huge sheet of glass from the garage roof moved in the brilliant moonlight. Sydney pulled at it and from underneath rose a very tall policeman with a long beard, very drunk. He said he had no legs. To assure him he was standing on them, I pulled up his trousers. In his relief, he danced down the street holding Sydney's hand. [*He was Stanley Grimm, the painter, a special constable.*]

Back at 97. Windows out and many holes – but all was well. Sydney left. Changed – out again – amazing sight – brilliant moon – blazing wreckage – glass, glass everywhere – ambulances and cars with flat tyres – carried a dog home.

April 17th, 1941, Thursday.
Woke after 2 hours sleep on a pile of cushions in the hall. The dog had left – the all-clear sounded. Thank God for a gloriously sunny morning. At 6 am, all skylights blown in – the sun poured through the holes in the roof. Everywhere is inches of dust and fallen plaster. Everyone very active and full of life.

Spent a long time getting to Piccadilly with Terence. Houses in Jermyn Street, Leicester Square still blazing. Back again to Cheyne Walk. Red roses from S. Up on the roof helping with the black-outs. To the ambulance station at 4 – now a strange devastating sight. No Chelsea Old Church. No Blue Café [*The Lombard Café was confused with the Blue Cockatoo, which survived*] – just a long stretch of debris. Hard to believe it is real.

Met Alec McTavish [*from King's Parade*] working with the demolition party. They had just found two more men standing on their heads – one, old Barton, who I had been looking for that morning with his son. Spent evening re-equipping ambulances and "picketing" in the street. Slept in my tin hat.

• • •

April 18th, 1941, Friday.
Short warning during the night. Back at 97. Greeted by Ric on a flying visit to find out the worst. Poor Ric.

Editor's note: "Poor Ric" was Richard Stewart-Jones, a young member of the Chelsea Society who had constituted himself a sort of one-man National Trust for the preservation of Chelsea's heritage. When he found that not only had the Old Church been bombed, but that looters were carrying away bricks and lead, he had the site fenced in. He later organised a huge campaign to get permission from the reluctant Diocesan authorities to rebuild. The day this permission came through in 1947, he got together a party of volunteer bricklayers who began the work with their bare hands.

The history of the church, its destruction, rebuilding and, finally, its reconsecration in 1958 is told in *Chelsea Old Church, the Church that Refused to Die* by Alan Russett and Tom Pocock, published by Historical Publications in 2004.

A memorial plaque by Reynold Stone commemorating "Poor Ric's" early death can be seen today in the church he loved.

1982

CHELSEA AT WAR

Incident Report

———

J. Trevor Williams, Duty Officer

When the 40th anniversary of the Second World War was commemorated in 1985, older Chelsea people who had lived here at that time remembered the Blitz and the V-weapons. One of them, Mr. E. A. Wheatley of Lawrence Street, who served in Civil Defence as a boy, showed us the log-book of the duty officer in the Borough Control Room, Mr. J. Trevor Williams, and turned to the entries for 16th April, 1941, thereafter known as "The Wednesday". That was the night when Chelsea Old Church was bombed.

For those unfamiliar with the abbreviations, their meanings are as follows:

DW – District Warden; DDW – Deputy District Warden; 10 – Incident Officer; XR – Express Report; RSD – Rescue Squad (Demolition); UXB – Unexploded Bomb; lB – Incendiary Bomb; AFS – Auxiliary Fire Service.

20.58.	Air Raid Message – Yellow.
21.05.	Air Raid Warning – Red.
21.28.	Flares reported south of river by Post B.
21.34.	Flares over Lots Road – by Post B.
21.40.	Flares south of river.
21.45.	DW Hanstown reports flares other side of Victoria.
22.35.	DW Hanstown reports big fire between them and Victoria.
23.29.	Post K report Wardens saw one falling. Hit Chelsea Gate, Royal Hospital. AFS called. Fire.
23.32.	DW Hanstown reports cloud of black smoke near Royal Hospital Infirmary. Hit, Caversham Street – Tite Street. South part Tite Street badly damaged. Casualties trapped. Tommy Wallis says major incident.

23.40. DDW Hanstown reports casualties trapped, 25 Cheyne Place. Incident Officer on job.

23.45. Post K reports several ambulances required Royal Hospital. Gate nearest end of Tite Street best approach. Many casualties. Queer object with wires attached at junction of Redesdale Street.

23.50. DDW Hanstown reports escape of gas opposite No. 25 Cheyne Place. He says he can't send XR – damage too widespread.

23.55. Daley, No.1 of 20 Squad, reports ambulances urgently required. One very bad spine case.

23.58. DDW Hanstown reports 25, 29, 31, 33, 35 Cheyne Place badly damaged. Approx. 70 casualties trapped. Amb. and Rescue required.

23.59. DW Hanstown reports flares over Victoria. Something dropped close to them while he was talking.

00.20. Royal Hospital Infirmary reported 40 trapped casualties. No amb. arrived. One RSD only arrived.

00.40. Royal Hospital requests ambulances to take away old people. One man 101 years. All shock cases.

00.45. Rang K for information *re* Rest Centres. They are sending people to Marlborough schools and Park Walk schools.

00.56. Officer from Chelsea Barracks requests more ambulances for Royal Hospital.

01.00. End of mine found in Shawfield Street and taken to Hall of Remembrance. About 50 casualties at one time in Hall of Remembrance, but they have been sorted out and distributed to Rest Centres.

01.10. Lansdell (F South) reports that about 41 sitting cases have been cleared from Hall of Remembrance to St. Luke's Hospital and Marlborough Schools. End of mine has hinge with ropes attached, not silken cords.

01.20. DDW Hanstown reports. Royal Hospital Infirmary reputed 40 trapped. Cheyne Place, 25. Nos. 29, 31, 33, 35 badly damaged and collapsed. Caversham Street backs of houses. One dead in 17. Evans, Incident Officer.

01.25. Rang D to confirm Danvers Street ambulance station mishap. Told to get off line for XR.

01.30. Post B confirms Old Church hit, and debris extends to King's Road.

01.35. Ring D *re* damage to Danvers Street. Report every body on their heads over Chelsea Old Church incident.

01.45. Squad-Leader Daley rang from Royal Hospital for Mr Horton.

01.55. Post D rang confirming bomb on Chelsea Old Church, and Danvers Street ambulance station out of commission.

02.00. Blankets required for dead – Post K.

02.10. Rang D for sitting ambulance. Report that a minute baby has swallowed some dust, and is suffering from shock. Is at Post D.

02.11. Rang K, who confirm HE near Chelsea Bridge. Chelsea Bridge Road, 20 yards west. No casualties, but barriers required.

02.12. DW Hanstown rang for information of other Chelsea incidents. Asked him to confirm on behalf of Mr. Crandell if bomb was UXB, and, if so, how long after falling did it explode.

02.17. Post B rang saying lBs falling Chelsea Park Gardens to King's Road.

02.20. Post K report lBs falling over bombed area.

02.30. Post K report fire at S. end of Paradise Walk. AFS know, but report that hoses have run out.

02.41. Post K say they cannot confirm if there is a crater near Chelsea Bridge and they are at the fire at Paradise Walk, which is reaching considerable pro portions.

02.45. Post D say that they can keep the baby on request – until after the blitz.

02.49. DW Cheyne reports about 11 casualties Chelsea Old Church, and that he has been blasted out of his office.

1985

CHELSEA AT WAR

The Royal Hospital in 1944-45

General Sir Clive Liddell

General Sir Clive Liddell has been good enough to send the following note on the Royal Hospital and the bombardment it sustained on the night of January 3rd, 1945:

Last December, with the end of the war in sight, it seemed possible that the Royal Hospital might be spared further damage. Such incidents as had occurred in 1944 had been of a comparatively trivial character. Thus in January a bomb had fortunately just missed the Nurses' Home and buried itself without exploding; and the following month some incendiary bombs had burned out harmlessly in the southern part of the grounds. In March a faulty anti-aircraft shell exploded in Ranelagh Gardens, while in June another wrecked the cloakroom and adjoining premises of my own house. Flying bombs luckily missed us, though their blast broke windows and did other minor damage on several occasions, notably on the 3rd July, when Sloane Court East was hit.

Our good fortune did not extend into 1945, as great devastation was caused on the 3rd January by a rocket bomb that fell on the North Front within a few feet of the north-east wing. This wing had been damaged so badly by a 500 lb. bomb in February 1918 that two-thirds of it had had to be rebuilt. The rocket completely wrecked the remainder of the original building as well as most of the reconstructed portion. Two officers and two ladies were killed outright, as was also an In-Pensioner who happened to be in the Chapel at the time. A third officer was severely wounded, and there were eighteen other casualties, some of whom had miraculous escapes. The death roll would undoubtedly have been higher had not some of the residents in this wing been away, attending the funeral of another officer who had overstrained himself during the air raids of 1941.

The work of rescue was carried out most efficiently by the Civil Defence of the Borough, assisted by American soldiers and others who happened to be in the neighbourhood and volunteered their aid. All the buildings in Light Horse Court were damaged to a greater or less extent, and it proved necessary to evacuate all the pensioners from the East Wing. Some went on furlough, while others were sent to the two country houses at Ross-on-Wye that had been taken over some years earlier. As a temporary measure, in view of the shortage of accommodation, no more old soldiers are being admitted to the Royal Hospital, and our numbers are now about one hundred less than in normal times.

Apart from the grievous loss of life this untoward incident has robbed the Royal Hospital of two of its historic residences. Some of the rooms destroyed had retained their original Wren panelling, while others had been redecorated by Robert Adam or Sir John Soane. One house had been occupied at different times by Dr. Bland, a friend of Walpole and later Provost of Eton, by the Rev. W. Barnard, father of Dr. Johnson's friend, the Bishop of Limerick, and in 1787-98 by Dr. Charles Burney. There the celebrated musician wrote the final volumes of his *History of Music*, and there his daughter Fanny lived for two years before her marriage. The flat on the second floor of the adjoining building which Dr. Burney occupied from 1798 until his death, is badly damaged, but it is hoped that it may be restored. Repairs are being effected gradually as labour becomes available, but some years must necessarily elapse before the Royal Hospital is completely reconstructed and refurnished.

Wrecked wing of Royal Hospital, Chelsea, 1944

CHELSEA AT WAR

We Shall Remember...

Tom Pocock

Excitement or fear? Which was the jolt that hit us when the siren whooped beside Albert Bridge? Probably a combination of the two. At first, excitement, mostly; particularly in a boy, as I was. Then, as the bombing continued, night after night, the component of fear grew. I was lucky; I had missed the Blitz, only being in Chelsea for the bombing of 1944 and the rockets of 1945. But perhaps I was not so lucky for it had been an historic and heroic time.

Such thoughts came to mind when, on 3rd. September, 1992, the Mayor of the Royal Borough, Councillor Elizabeth Christmas, unveiled the war memorial plaque to the 457 civilians killed in Chelsea. At once she established a bond with the older members of the crowd on Dovehouse Green: members of her own family had been killed by the bombing over the border in Kensington.

The plaque, designed by Teresa Elwes, the daughter of the custodian of Carlyle's house, from a concept by David Le Lay, and carved from Portland stone, was unveiled on the fifty-third anniversary of the outbreak of the Second World War and that anniversary alone would have been enough to bring back memories to those of us old enough to have them of that time.

During the war, every Londoner had a "bomb story". They have faded now, of course, but on this day some of them were brought out of the attics of memory. One woman remembered seeing the windows of Cheyne Walk sucked outward by blast; another, the open expanse of night sky that showed that the tower of the Old Church was no longer there; a third, who had been living in the Royal Hospital, of the sudden darkness when the V2 rocket exploded. I had shared a memory of that morning; looking back from a No.11 bus as the explosion seemed to blow people down the street like autumn leaves.

By that time, those who had endured the earlier Blitz in Chelsea were the honoured veterans. They could tell tales of the disasters when shelters were hit – in Beaufort Street and in the crypt of the Church of the Holy Redeemer, for example; of the bombing of Sloane Square station, where, they said, the blazing abyss had looked like the mouth of hell; and always the night the Old Church was destroyed (to rise again after a decade). There were the heroes and heroines we knew: the tireless Dr. Costello, who worked on when his family was killed; Bert Thorpe, who died with the women and children he was comforting at the Holy Redeemer; Dorothy Quick, the intelligent spinster, who worked throughout as a telephonist on the A.R.P. (Air Raid Precautions) switchboard at the Town Hall and never recovered from the strain of those months, and many more. Then there are the dead, whose names are inscribed by the Commonwealth War Graves Commission in the Roll of Honour at Westminster Abbey: robust names from old Middlesex, double-barrelled names from Cheyne Walk and Hans Town, cockney names, literary names and theatrical names; all social strata and all income groups; the whole marvellous social mixture of Chelsea as it was and, occasionally, still is.

Then there is the exact memory of what it was like, difficult to bring back into focus at first. Remember walking towards Chelsea after dark, early in 1944, down the middle of Buckingham Palace Road – for there was no traffic. The siren wails and the pulse quickens. Is there time to get home before it starts? There should be five or ten minutes. The pace quickens and you look up at the sky to the south. At first there is nothing, then the wavering lights of distant searchlights shining on clouds. Two or three minutes later, again far to the south, there is a sparkle of flak in the dark and then a faint thumping. Now you have reached Royal Hospital Road. Perhaps you look around for some substantial arch, or doorway under which to shelter from falling shell-splinters once the barrage starts.

Then the London searchlights switch on: a stockade of brilliant white beams, waving to and fro, then concentrating in cones: at an apex, something like a silver moth – a German bomber. Up climbs the tracer in streams of red beads. Higher, the darkness is splashed with shell-bursts of flame. The noise merges into a continuous thundering: the throb of aeroengines, the heavy thump of bombs, the *bang* of guns and the *pang* of shell-bursts, the crackle of light flak and finally the *whoosh* of the great rocket-battery in Battersea Park. Look westward across Chelsea. A bomber is caught in the searchlights. Perhaps it is going for Lots Road power-station, or the bridges. A billow of red-lit smoke erupts, silhouetting the rooftops: that was its bomb-load. Next morning, you hear that those bombs hit the Guinness flats. Then the memory cuts out like the end of a film-clip; for others there will be memories of digging in the smoking rubble and carrying blood-soaked bundles in blankets.

It has all become something of a blur with flashes in sharp focus. But facts help and these are in the records of the old Chelsea Borough Council, dated 24th. October, 1945, when it was all over. Chelsea – the original Chelsea – covered 660 acres and the wartime population averaged 30, 000. Between the bursting of the first bomb on Chelsea on 27th. August, 1940, and the impact of the V2 on the Royal Hospital on 3rd. January, 1945, it was hit by 321 missiles and thousands of incendiary bombs. These killed 534 people – 77 of them in the armed forces – and wounded 1,565: 842 of them seriously and, in addition, "a very large number" were treated for shock. If you were living in Chelsea at the time, your chance of being killed or wounded was more than one in 15.

It all happened half a century ago, but it is important that we do not forget and so the memorial on Dovehouse Green is a quiet reminder. [1992]

Royal Hospital

CHELSEA AT WAR

...and Others are Remembered, Too

Colin McIntyre

The most interesting of the war memorials built after the Great War of 1914-1918 are the village and parish-based ones which list the full names of those commemorated and the units they served in. Although by 1914, Chelsea could no longer be considered a village, most of its memorials were very much on a parish basis. They thus serve as magnificent primary sources for the views of all those who were mature in the early 1920's. They tell us something of their attitudes towards war, religion, patriotism, class, and community life. Studied carefully, they give us a picture of a society and community-living now almost completely lost.

Although it is the 1914-18 war memorials that have most to tell us about our immediate military and social history, Chelsea has other memorials from earlier days. Supreme among these, of course, is the Royal Hospital itself. Built on the orders of Charles II, designed by Sir Christopher Wren, it still stands as a working tribute to British soldiers.

Not all those killed in war, died on active service abroad. A marble plaque by the chapel entrance tells a unique story:

Royal Hospital Chelsea
In Memory of Those Officers, In-Pensioners and Residents of the Royal Hospital, named hereon, who Lost Their Lives within the Precincts by Enemy Action in two Wars.

It lists those killed on the 16th. February, 1918: Captain Ernest Ludlow MC, Captain of Invalids, late of the Grenadier Guards, his wife, two sons and a niece. Twenty-three years later, on the 16th. April, 1941 German bombs killed four nurses, the Wardmaster and eight In-Pensioners; and then again on 3rd. January, 1945 another five of those living at the Royal Hospital when the V2 rocket struck.

Another early monument of war in Chelsea is the tall obelisk in

Royal Hospital Gardens, to 255 officers and men of the XXIV'th Regiment who fell at Chilianwalla on 14th. January 1849. This battle in the Second British-Sikh war was somewhat indecisive. Although a British-Indian Force of 12,000 men under Lord Gough drove a much larger Sikh force under Shir Singh from the field of battle, they lost 2,300 in killed and wounded, and had to retire from the field owing to a shortage of water. It is interesting to note that the dead include three lieutenant-colonels, and that all the names on the column are listed in strict order of rank.

This hierarchical practice is followed in the Boer War memorial to VI Dragoon Guards (The Carabiniers) on the Chelsea Embankment by Chelsea Bridge, erected in 1905 to men who fell in South Africa between 1899-1902. Chelsea's main 20th-century war memorial is the Cross in Sloane Square, modelled on the Cross of Sacrifice by Reginald Blomfield R.A.

Chelsea does not seem to have had a specific unit of its own, other than the Middlesex Regiment. The Duke of York's Headquarters in the King's Road was home to the second of the London divisions of the Territorial Force, 47th. (2nd. London) Division. But Chelsea men would serve in London battalions in both divisions, as would Irishmen from all over London in the London Irish Rifles, the only battalion of the London Regiment whose peacetime drill hall was in Chelsea, at the Duke of York's H.Q. itself. Artillery, engineers, transport columns, medical units were also based on the Duke of York's H.Q., but as far as I know, none of them bore the word Chelsea in their titles.

To find details of the units in which the men of Chelsea served we have to look to those church rolls of honour which record more than the names of those who died; or to individual plaques put up by parents on the church walls. Sadly, the complete list of Chelsea's Great War dead which was apparently compiled by the Chelsea Town Clerk at the time of the appeal for funds for the Sloane Square memorial, appears to have been lost when Chelsea was subsumed into Kensington, for the Borough's senior librarian could find no trace of it in 1990. Luckily, most of the names can be found in the parish churches: 81 names in the fine War Memorial Chapel at Holy Trinity, Sloane Street; another 52 names at St. Simon Zelotes, Cadogan Square, etc. In the Hall of Remembrance in Flood Street, the 83 names of those who died from Christ Church parish are recorded in alphabetical order, with only name and initials given. Chelsea is also home to the principal Church of Scotland church in London – St. Columba's in Pont Street. This, as might be expected, was the home church of the London Scottish, officially the 14th. (County of London) Bn. of the London Regiment. It has remained so for all successor London Scottish (TA) formations.

Chelsea Old Church is the oldest church in Chelsea, but it was not a parish church when the Great War memorials were being built. It was a Chapel of Ease. Sadly its time for memorials came in the Second World War, when parachute mines almost destroyed it in 1941. A memorial plaque placed inside the porch after the rebuilding tells the story:

The present building replaces that bombed on the night of 16 April* 1941 when five fire-watchers were killed

Henry Frankland
Yvonne Gree
Michael Hodge
Sidney Sims
Frederick Winter

in whose Memory this Stone is erected.

Carved in stone or painted on wood, the names, fighting man and civilian alike, remind us of past grief and pride.

1992

Memorial on Dovehouse Green

*Actually it was at 1:15 a.m. on 17th April.

CHELSEA AT WAR

At Last We Remembered Them

—

Tom Pocock

One man's mission is fulfilled in Chelsea.

Just after a quarter to eight on the morning of 3rd July, 1944, Turk's Row and Sloane Court East, just off Lower Sloane Street, presented a busy scene. American soldiers were trooping out of the flats, where they were billeted, and into the street where lorries waited to take them to their day's work. A few were women and most belonged to 130 Chemical Processing Company, which was being held in London in readiness for an outbreak of gas warfare with Germany as the Second World War reached its climax, for the Allies had landed in Normandy less than a month before.

At that moment the jet engine of a V1, launched from the Pas de Calais cut out over the Thames and the flying-bomb began its sharp descent into Chelsea. It dived steeply over Ranelagh Gardens and

The devastation in Sloane Court East and Turks Row on July 3rd 1944

the ton of high explosive in its nose-cone exploded at the junction of Sloane Court East and Turk's Row.

An eighteen-year-old Chelsea boy, Bill Figg, heard the explosion. He was on his way home while in the process of transferring from the RAF to the Army and he hurried towards the rising cloud of smoke and dust to be one of the first on the scene. What he saw remained fixed in his memory: the wrecked buildings, spilling their walls, ceilings and contents into the street; the smashed lorries; and the broken bodies. When the heavy rescue team arrived they estimated that seventy-four Americans and at least three civilians – some said ten – had been killed; among the dead was a Canadian officer, also billeted in the flats.

Londoners were being killed by the hundred that summer, there was strict censorship – particularly as to the sites of what were called 'incidents' so as to confuse the enemy's aim – and this horror quickly passed into history. It would be remembered by those who had lived in Chelsea at the time that a lot of Americans had been killed in Lower Sloane Street but it was not publicly recorded. When, in 1991, the Chelsea Society erected a memorial plaque in Dovehouse Green, that commemorated Chelsea's 457 civilian dead of the Second World War but not those in the armed forces of the Allies.

It then seemed that the only Londoner who remembered the event of 3rd July 1944 was Bill Figg. He had become an electrical engineer and his hobby was local history and the photographing of the changing Chelsea scene. But his memory of 1944 and what he planned to do about it was more than a hobby, it was a dedication. He was determined to find out more about the Americans who had died that morning. He found contemporary Civil Defence reports and a list of casualties names. But his efforts to discover more about the unit to which they belonged – its name and number had never been published – by writing to authorities in Washington drew a blank. He received sympathetic replies – including several from the White House – but either the question was referred elsewhere, or he was told that one terrible incident among so many did not warrant either the time and effort in research, or the allocation of funds for specific commemoration.

Eventually Bill Figg came to a conclusion. He himself would arrange the commemoration. So, during 1998, he completed what seemed to be all the research that was possible, himself designed and had made the stone memorial plaque and paid for it; with the help of friends, he arranged for guards of honour from the

The service conducted by the Rev. Prebendary Leighton Thomson

Territorial Army, pensioners from the Royal Hospital and the British Legion, standard-bearers and buglers to attend an unveiling ceremony.

Initially, the United States Embassy agreed to send officers from its staff together with a chaplain; then, hearing that a small metal memorial disc had been set in the pavement of Turk's Row by an American citizen in 1997, they felt their presence was unnecessary and withdrew. However, the Mayor of the Royal Borough, Councillor Dr. Jonathan Munday, agreed to unveil the memorial and the Rev. Prebendary Leighton Thomson, the former vicar of Chelsea Old Church, agreed to conduct a short service.

And so it was that on the afternoon of Sunday, 4th October, the police cordoned off Turk's Row – probably for the first time since July, 1944 – and a crowd collected. The ceremony that followed – the military parade, the prayers, the speeches, the Last Post and Reveille bugle calls and the unveiling was an event to remember. Usually such occasions are the consequence of official action by government or council; rarely are they the result of one individual's dedication. This ceremony grew from the grass-roots of Chelsea. Fifty-four years on, Bill Figg's terrible memory flowered in a generous and moving act of commemoration.

1998

CHELSEA AT WAR

After

John Watney

I returned from the wars, as the saying goes, more or less intact, and took, in 1946, a small room in Bywater Street. The little houses in this cul-de-sac were the worse for wear and tear after six years of war-time neglect. There was a veterinary surgeon's animal hospital at the end of the street, which was so under-staffed that when owner's brought their pets for treatment they had to "do it" themselves.

A few yards round the corner in the King's Road, stood the Markham Arms, a well-known meeting place for artists and writers. It was an old-fashioned Victorian building, and had a Public Bar, where beer was a penny cheaper than in the Private Bar. Sandwiched between these two, and completely screened off was a narrow Ladies' Bar. The walls of this discreet enclosure contained louvres which could be pressed open from inside so that the ladies taking refuge there could keep an eye on what was going on in the other bars, and receive the occasional port that a gallant gentleman might offer. Although only women were allowed in the Ladies' Bar, they could, if they wished, enter the other two bars. Girls did, but elderly ladies who believed that it was unladylike to be seen in a general bar, preferred the anonymity of the Ladies' Bar.

The whole edifice was controlled by Mrs. Andrews. Ma Andrews was a solid lady, who had a face that looked as if it were made of brown paper which had been scrumpled up and put hurriedly together again. She did not serve drinks herself but sat on a sort of throne at the back of the bar to keep an eye on the barmaids and to decide whether or not to cash a cheque or enter on a huge black slate the drinks of someone who had come out without any money. She had violent likes and dislikes, and would not hesitate to throw out anyone she did not like. On the other hand she would do anything for those she did like. Such a one was Sir John Squire, poet and sometime editor of the *London Mercury*.

Jack Squire was mad about cricket. Before the war he had taken part in the famous cricket match at Fordcombe, which A. G. Macdonald described in his book *England, Their England*. Jack was determined to revive the cricket team and with the help of Patrick Howarth, a demobilised Intelligence Officer and budding author, cajoled, threatened and persuaded sundry characters to join the team. He called it "The Markham Arms Cricket Club". A fact that so delighted Ma Andrews, that whenever the team set forth she would slip Pat Howarth £40 "to keep the teams' spirits up", as she put it.

Although Jack Squire had a considerable range of acquaintances and friends, he always had great difficulty in getting eleven "good men and true" on to the cricket field at any one moment. Sometimes there would be real cricketers. I remember that when we played Meopham in Kent, we fielded Percy Fender who also played for England. Sometimes Jack would recruit an auther like Nigel Balchin who was also a county player; and Pat Howarth was reasonably proficient. But the rest of us were of very doubtful value.

One was a Russian painter whom Jack had recruited at the Chelsea Arts Club called Sosonov. Sos and I were last and one but last batsmen, and as he approached the wicket, he said, "What do I do?" There wasn't much time to explain the whole game to him, so I told him to stand in front of the stumps and hold his bat in front of him; which he did, looking rather like the sentry at Pompeii waiting for the molten ash to engulf him. As it happened I was bowled to a cow-shot, so that Sos retired from his one and only cricket match with the commendable score of: 0 not out.

One of our keenest players was in fact a Cambridge rowing blue called Bertie Boret. He, like Jack Squire, liked to anchor himself in a quiet corner of the out-field. Unfortunately for Bertie, we once played an eleven, whose cricket field was perched on a hill. A road ran from the field's boundary down to a small stream. Bertie had, as usual, anchored himself in this remote part, unaware that the local opposition, aware of the existence of the road, invariably aimed their shots in his direction. There was a bye-law that on that side of the field there was no boundary line, so that while Berie trotted, puffing, up and down the hill, the local batsmen scored seven or eight runs. He was so incensed, and exhausted, by this, that he engaged a local youth with a bicycle to do the running and fetching, and this saved himself much breath, and cut down the local run-getting from seven to three.

We had to bring an umpire and two scorers. The scorers were girl-friends, but the umpire was Robin Green, an archaeologist, who spent most of his time paddling around Chelsea Reach looking for medieval coins. His umpiring was somewhat erratic as he used these coins to count the number of balls in an over. On one occasion he disappeared completely during the tea break so the match went on without him; until an irate woman stormed on to the field, and said that one of our cricketers was digging up her cabbages. Jack rushed to the woman's garden, and there, sure enough, was Robin digging up her cabbages.

"You mustn't dig up this poor lady's cabbages," said Jack.

"Cabbages be dammed," said Robin, "there's a wonderful medieval dump under here."

Jack, always kind, bought all the cabbages from the poor woman, and we trudged back to Chelsea each of us carrying a cabbage.

We never won a single match, but this did not dampen Ma Andrews' interest in what she referred to as "my cricket club".

Acquiring food was a greater problem than getting paint and canvasses. Rationing was still in force and very few of the studios, such as those in Glebe Place and Trafalgar Studios, had adequate, if any, cooking facilities.

Indeed, it was cheaper and easier, especially if you had children, to eat out in one or the other of the numerous little restaurants that lived on, as far as one could see, almost nothing, all over Chelsea. There was Caletta's in the King's Road. It was staffed by incredibly old waiters dressed in black morning coats, striped trousers, starched "dickies" and cuffs on which they calculated, with a stub of a pencil, the bill. The menu consisted of one dish: spaghetti and mince, which was usually rabbit or even the awful whale-meat, a hang-over from the war, but at least for a few shillings you could feed the whole family, and the atmosphere was always happy.

Down by the river there was the Blue Cockatoo, which was more of a bun-house than a restaurant, and a favourite rendezvous place for artists and writers. Close by was the Pier Hotel which had a restaurant on the first floor where businessmen would take authors and artists to discuss contracts. The tables were set by the large Georgian windows with a beautiful view of the bridge and the river.

Another favourite place was the Queen's Restaurant off Sloane Square. It was run by a cheerful Italian family and consisted of two large rooms. The first room which led in from the square was an ordinary-looking place catering for the normal passers-by. It was the second, inner room that was interesting. It was reached by an arch-way, and in its rather dark interior – it appeared to have no windows – there were only two or three large round tables. The one on the right was Augustus John's table. The celebrated painter presided over a number of admirers, mainly female.

Opposite was the Journalist's Table. This was usually presided over by Brian Chapman, who was then an editor of the *Daily Express*, and lived nearby. The unusual feature of the Journalist's Table was that the meals were paid for by those journalists who were working, and not by those who had been sacked or were "resting". The turnover of staff in Fleet Street was so considerable at that time that editors and sub-editors hardly dared go out for lunch for fear of finding a hard-faced man sitting at their desk, and saying, "Yes, and what can I do for you?"

Another refuge was The Pheasantry at 152 Kings Road. It consisted of an amalgam of large working studios. In one of them Hein Heckroth designed the sets for the film *The Red Shoes* with Moira Shearer in the leading role. In the basement was a small restaurant that was originally created to cater for the appetites of the artists working in the studios above.

It was run by a fiery, shock-haired Italian called Remy, who had a somewhat unorthodox view of the financial running of a club. He would charge nothing to indigent artists, particularly if they had children, for a meal, and treble to successful or wealthy artists and visitors. Next to the first room, which had a bar, was a second room which had a minute dance floor (music supplied by an ancient wind-up gramophone), and here he would charge a stiff "dancing fee"; so that you could either sit and have a cheap meal, or if you felt like dancing, pay a fee.

Remy himself would often have a meal there with some friend of his. One of his close friends was the singer Mario Lanza. Whenever Mario Lanza was having dinner with Remy you could expect a drastic change from the old records that Remy usually supplied; Mario had a habit of singing at the top of his voice which would effectually drown the tinkling of the gramophone and make the diners think they were going deaf.

Chelsea seemed to be teeming with artists. There was Matthew Smith, a mild-looking man who painted very lurid compositions. On the other hand, there was Sir Alfred Munnings, who painted horses. Munnings hated Stanley Spencer, who painted resurrection scenes, and apparently reported little Spencer for painting grossly indecent pictures. Whether he ever, in fact, did so is open to dispute but the Chelsea intellectuals thought so and that was enough to bring the artists and their supporters out in strength.

One day, Sir Alfred was scheduled to address a meeting at Chelsea Town Hall. His critics assembled outside in the King's Road to barrack and hoot at him. Many of the demonstrators appeared on horseback. Some of the girl demonstrators dressed in almost as scanty attires as the famous Lady Godiva. The King's Road was completely blocked with semi-nude horsewomen and enthusiastic pro-Spencer supporters. The police were out in force stopping the traffic from interfering with the commendable demonstration, and preventing outside forces from interfering with what was essentially an important, if private, dispute among artists.

Not far away, in Old Church Street, was the Chelsea Arts Club, favoured by James McNeill Whistler at the end of the nineteenth century, which carried on the controversy while it's members played snooker. The club was still an exclusively male artists' establishment and was known locally as The Hospital, for it succoured artists in distress. Each member had a key to the front door, and if thrown out of their homes by their womenfolk, which seemed to happen quite frequently to painters, they let themselves into the club, and finding an empty bedroom quietly put themselves to bed and rested peacefully until woken by the smell of bacon-and-eggs telling them that the club's excellent breakfast was ready.

It was here that the annual Chelsea Arts Ball at the Albert Hall on New Year's Eve was conceived and planned under the energetic inspiration of a handsome sculptor called Loris Reay, who would on the Eve itself lead the cortege of floats usually dressed as a Roman emperor. The floats, beautifully constructed during the year had a short life. As soon as the parade was over and the New Year rung in they were torn to pieces by the hundreds of costumed revellers; and Loris would return to the club and start planning next year's Chelsea Arts Ball.

He hoped that it would go on forever, but the invaders were already on the move. The first to arrive in Chelsea were the smart little restaurants which served up French and Italian dishes. They quickly took over from the cheap-eating places such as Caletta's and The Unity. The next were home-hungry young couples who saw in the dilapidated working studios, ideal homes – once, of course, they had been modernised. Finally came the trendy boutiques from Carnaby Street, who quickly took over any existing vacant shops. The artists fled, many of them to addresses around Finsbury Park, where there were large, empty houses with huge rooms that could be quickly adapted as studios.

Chelsea never changes. Seventy-five years ago, my mother and father had a house in Walpole Street. He was an apprentice architect in Sir Edwin Lutyen's office, until the war came to drive him into the Services. She was an artist. So, naturally, they wanted to live in Chelsea. This has continued ever since. Creative people, whether painters, writers, restaurateurs or boutique owners, have always gyrated to Chelsea, and will no doubt continue to do so within the foreseeable future.

1990

Chelsea Arts Club in the First World War

———

Tom Cross

In August, 1914, the long peace of Europe ended and no one in England could foresee the crippling effect that this would have upon the social fabric of the nation. In London, the sculptor Derwent Wood, supported by several leading members formally proposed that a Chelsea Arts Club Corps be formed and sought the sanction of the War Office for this. He hoped for at least one hundred members and was sure that "the Club would be proud to have made such an effort in the present crisis". When Alfred Munnings came to London from Cornwall at the outbreak of war he found fellow members, who had already joined the Artists' Rifles, solemnly drilling with broomsticks in the garden. He went to the nearest recruiting station in Chelsea but to his surprise he was rejected from the Yeomanry because of his blind eye and returned to Hampshire to paint hop-pickers.

The older artists, too old for active service, helped as best they could. They turned their studios into workshops, or they patrolled the streets as special constables, prepared to cope with any emergency. The landscape painter Arthur Black was sent to France to make hand and foot splints for the wounded. William Dickson was also too old for the Army, but, being a good mechanic, he turned his studio in the King's Road into a workshop and for three years devoted all his time to making fine parts for the sights of field-guns.

In the early days of the war, the Commandant of the 3rd London General Hospital made an impassioned plea in the bar of the Club for help with the medical services and, as a consequence, some thirty members joined the Royal Army Medical Corps. Many of these enlisted in 1914 and stayed, although past military age, until the end of the war. When Derwent Wood joined the R.A.M.C. in 1915 he was the first sculptor to be recruited into the Army to practise his art. He helped the wounded and disfigured in the field, by making silver masks to cover facial wounds. Others drove ambulances or served as stretcher-bearers for the Red Cross throughout the war in France, Belgium, Italy and the Balkans.

Henry Tonks, then teaching at the Slade School, combined his medical experience with his artistic skills in an extraordinary way. At the beginning of the war, Tonks, then fifty-nine, served in England as a volunteer hospital orderly but by January, 1915, he was in France and the following year was made a lieutenant in the R.A.M.C. He became interested in the recording of facial surgery cases and began to visit the Cambridge Military Hospital where Sir Harold Gillies had developed techniques of skin grafting to repair soldiers' disfigured faces. He worked with Gillies in the operating theatre recording operations and made a series of remarkable pastel drawings of severely wounded soldiers.

In the last year of the war Tonks was appointed a war artist, agreed to tackle a medical subject and, after much indecision, he left for France in June, 1918, in the company of John Singer Sargent, to paint a field dressing-station for propaganda purposes. With the war still at its height, he worked on studies in an advanced dressing-station near to the front line, although with typical self-depreciation he wrote "anybody less suited to be a special artist probably does not exist". However, he went on, "I pride myself that it gives a reasonable account of modern war surgery… I used to make such notes as I could of actual wounded men and I think most of what I saw is based on actual fact."

Gaps were appearing in the Club as members were called into the armed forces and, of the 319 members, 74 were serving with the

The Chelsea Arts Club

Colours by 1916. They were all made honorary members and their subscription was waived, their photographs were exhibited in the Club and food parcels were sent to them at the Front. As far as possible the Club tried to proceed with its normal affairs but attendance was down and income was reduced. There was concern that members would not find employment as artists and it was agreed to put on a cheap lunch at one shilling instead of one and sixpence. It was also agreed that any artist who was in receipt of help from the Artists' Benevolent Fund should be allowed three months credit for meals but although every economy was being made, the Club was running at a loss. Because of the lack of young men, the red-coated waiters were replaced by waitresses, the cost of wines and spirits was raised, economy was made in the use of coal and electric light and the Club closed at 11 p.m.

In 1914, a new Club steward was appointed, a young man called Albert William Smith, who, for no good reason, was immediately christened 'John the Steward'. He was then about 24 years old, courteous and well-spoken and had trained as a servant. His young wife Ellen Mayne became stewardess. 'John' soon became a Club institution. He recalled the casual atmosphere of the Club on his first days:

"I arrived this morning, 2nd. April, 1914, at the Club, on Good Friday. Most of the members were away, being holiday time, so I did not see many the first day… On Monday most of the members came back and dinner seemed a strange affair after private service. I thought what a strange lot of people to be sure. Members 'lazed' on the table, swore a bit, and had not brushed their hair, but it is easy to fall into line. I mean there was no need to be embarrassed. Mr. Robert Fowler came in on the Saturday afternoon, and seeing that I was new, started showing me a few card tricks. Mr. George Coats came in and in his well modulated voice asked me my name, etc. At that time he was Chairman of the House Committee. The Annual Dinner followed on the 27th, a pleasant affair; English ribs of beef from Smithfield Market at 9d a pound, quite different from the 'War meat'. We managed to finish the clearing away by 2 a.m."

Together, the steward and stewardess ran the Club; their duties were comprehensive, overseeing everything from the kitchen and other staff to the wine cellar and tradesmen. After balls or dinners, they could be on duty in the bar until 4 a.m. and then be required to prepare 120 breakfasts before the last guests left. 'John' was a keen observer of the members. He admired their way of life, he enjoyed their successes and commiserated with their disappointments. He wrote his reminiscences in two journals, parts of which are quoted here. He described a Club which was boisterous, outgoing and friendly, yet at a time of war tensions were high, fierce disagreements could occur and members not infrequently came to blows:

"On Monday night the Club gave a dinner to Bill Baynes, and a riotous affair it was. Bill drank innumerable pints of beer, and sloe gin. After dinner the company went into the billiard room, where singing and a general carousal took place. One member happened to say that any person serving in France must be lousy. Bill Baynes instantly let down his trousers, pulled up his shirt and said 'Look at this and see if I am lousy.' Afterwards they patrolled the billiard room, headed by Bill, singing 'Ribs of beef and b----y great lumps of Duff'. This went on until two o'clock and, on the following day, Bill returned to France. Several members went to Victoria with him and jumped over the barrier to wish 'God Speed' to poor Sergeant Baynes; and that was the last we saw of him, as he was blown up by a shell three weeks afterwards."

Although many of the men were away, the Club was at its liveliest, there was constant coming and going of members on home leave, or others calling in between portrait commissions of the military.

Philip Wilson Steer was in the Special Constabulary for a short time, later he was recruited as a war artist on a scheme that was introduced by the Government in 1916. He was asked to paint Dover harbour for the Navy, however he found this disturbing to his comfort. Steer's requirements while painting (as listed by his friend Philip Connard) were: One, shelter from the wind (his fear of draughts was notorious). Two, proximity to a lavatory. Three, shade from the sun. Four, protection from children. Five, a suitable subject. These were not easily satisfied, he found his hotel accommodation

BARRY FANTONI

what I like about the C.A.C is that's itsh the only club you got thrown into for being drunk

depressing and when he started to paint in watercolour "some blighter comes up and wants to see my permit, which is very upsetting just in the middle of laying on a wash!" To add to his difficulties he found that "Ships and boats had a habit of moving unexpectedly and after spending much time and labour in putting one in, one finds one has got it in the wrong place."

H.M. Bateman, the *Punch* artist, had made an unsuccessful attempt to join the Army but after a brief period of training he contracted rheumatic fever and was invalided out. During his recovery he was in the 3rd London General Hospital, Wandsworth, where he found a number of friends from Chelsea. He decorated the recreation room with several cartoons, one of which was of Sgt. Derwent Wood fixing a splint to a straffed microbe.

William Orpen, Augustus John and John Sargent were the biggest names among the war artists. Some of the earliest commissions of the war were offered by the Canadian Government, as part of a scheme that had been pursued with energy by Lord Beaverbrook, and Orpen was one of the first major painters to be appointed. During his first months in France he was remarkably unproductive, objecting to being treated like a child, and being expected to show his work each day and to hear it criticised by philistine officers in terms which outraged him. He spent much time quarrelling with the authorities who thought he was "Irish and artistic". Orpen was later appointed an official war artist to the British in 1917 and was still in France in 1920.

Augustus John had been saved from the rigours of active service by an ailment he described as "housemaid's knee". He applied for a war artist appointment in 1917 and the Canadians offered him a major's commission with full pay. He came to France in January, 1918, to the area around Vimy and cut a dashing figure as the only bearded officer in the Army except for the King, for whom he was frequently mistaken. John greatly enjoyed the attention that he was given but was sent home in disgrace for knocking down a fellow officer.

The most ambitious picture to come from the Western Front, and one of the most powerful, was John Sargent's *Gassed*. A subject had been suggested to him by the War Office – the co-operation between American and British troops – and as an American living in London this appeared to be appropriate. It was suggested that this should be a "super-picture" designed, like John's, to be hung in a Hall of Remembrance, to be 20 ft. long by 9 ft. high. With a personal letter from Lloyd George, Sargent received V.I.P. treatment.

He arrived in France in July, 1917, and was given good accommodation with the Guards division on the Somme. He made many sketches, working under a large white umbrella – later camouflaged – and was taken on occasional rides in a tank. However he had great difficulty in finding a subject of sufficient gravity and importance to fill the large canvas, without it looking, he said "like an illustrated-paper kind of subject". Eventually Sargent chose to paint a scene that he had witnessed at Le-Bac-du-Sud on the road to Arras, where a temporary dressing-station had been set up to relieve the suffering of hundreds of men who had been temporarily blinded by mustard-gas. When completed, this haunting painting became one of the most famous of the war pictures.

Into the autumn of 1918 the war dragged on. But at last, in 1918, the Kaiser abdicated and two days later the German delegation signed the Armistice. In the Club, the celebrations were fierce and, on Armistice Day, Alfred Munnings arranged a dinner for which he decorated the billiard room. This was an uproarious affair with speeches and frequent interruptions for his own recitations and songs, his rendering of *The Raven* was interrupted by squalling cats on the roof and curses from himself.

Colonel John Cameron presided at the Peace Dinner. As the steward remembered; "Col. Cameron was very strict; some members were whispering during a speech and he jumped to his feet and said in broad Scotch, 'Will you shut up with your row down the room there!' After dinner, when the speeches were over about midnight, I saw him with his arm around a maid and when he saw me he said, 'You know John, you'll have to get a bit of discipline in this place.'"

Originally entitled, *A Rumbustious Century for The Chelsea Arts Club.*

1991

STANLEY HOUSE

David Le Lay

1991 is the tercentenary of the generally accepted date when Stanley House was built at the western end of the King's Road. However, Chelsea historians have tended to cast doubt on this date as being too early; yet, there is evidence to suggest that the house is actually older than 300 years.

There is a distinct tendency to call all historic buildings in the classical style either "Queen Anne" or, even more commonly, "Georgian". This omits to credit the considerable number of fine buildings, especially medium to small mansion houses, built during the reigns of Charles II and William & Mary, which are the very epitome of the English classical house.

One of the reasons for this anomaly is that many of these houses were subsequently "modernised". The 18th. century "window replacement industry" in particular was very active and managed to completely change the character of many of these buildings which has mislead future historians as to their real date. A notable Chelsea example is the Royal Hospital which, although it was built between 1682-92, can easily be mistaken for a Georgian building by those not knowing it was designed by Sir Christopher Wren. This is largely on account of its double-hung sash windows which were inserted by Robert Adam in the 1760's as a replacement for the original leaded-light mullioned and transomed casements.

Similarly, Stanley House has deceived many a scholar, including the author of Volume IV of *The Survey of London*, Walter Godfrey, who, in 1913, wrote "It would seem from the character of the architecture that the house in its present form was not erected until the reign of George 1" and "it is an excellent example of a Georgian house". Stanley House, like the Royal Hospital, has Georgian windows but that is all that is Georgian about it; in all other respects it is typical of a type of house built during the reign of Charles II (1660-89). The particular type to which Stanley House belongs is known as a "compact double-pile".

The characteristics of these houses, of which there are a surprisingly large number throughout the country, are that they have a square or rectangular plan whose dimensions are usually in multiples of 15 feet (Stanley House is a 45 foot square). This mathematical preoccupation with geometry is continued throughout the design which was always rigidly symmetrical, certainly so far as the external elevations were concerned, with usually a front door to both the entrance and the garden fronts. These houses have two principal floors of equal grandeur and importance (Georgian houses usually have only one *piano nobile*) the upper floor being reached by means of a spacious ceremonial staircase. The ground floor was raised upon a basement, normally containing kitchens and cellars, and there was an attic floor in the form of a hipped roof with dormer windows; all four floors being connected by the "back stairs". The hipped roof was surmounted by a leaded flat roof which was usually surrounded by a balustrade with an octagonal glazed cupola or lantern providing access and a crowning feature to the whole design. These houses were invariably built in prominent positions and such roof terraces enabled the owners to enjoy the view. As the balustrade and cupola were entirely of timber construction and especially vulnerable to the effects of the weather, only a few have survived. Stanley House has all of these characteristics and where the features no longer exist, there is substantial evidence to be found in the building itself that they did once exist.

These houses are often called "Restoration Houses" for they were built at a time of prosperity and confidence after the restoration of the monarchy in 1660. Their architectural inspiration came from designs of the 1630's by Inigo Jones. Influences can also be traced from France where Charles II had spent most of his exile and also Holland from where many Huguenot refugees came to this country at that time.

Chelsea's principal historian, Thomas Faulkner, tells us in his *Chelsea and its Environs* that Stanley House was built in about 1691, it was left in an unfinished state and unoccupied for several years. The date of 1691 is the year of the death of William Stanley who was the grandson of Sir Robert Stanley, second son of the sixth Earl of Derby. William Stanley was the last in that particular line of the Stanley family and as he had no direct heirs this would explain why the house remained unoccupied after his death. It was usual for people to build a new house for themselves either upon becoming married or inheriting. William Stanley inherited the family home, then known as "Brickhills", in 1676 and it is therefore most likely that he set about building Stanley House in the 1680's but that its internal fitting out was not completed when he died. This is borne

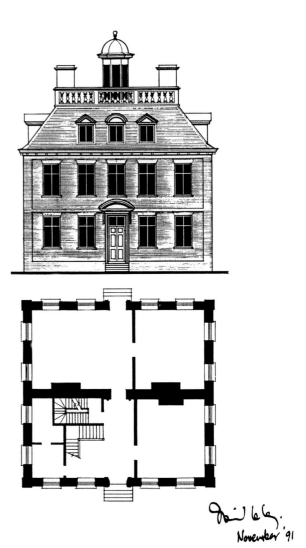

A reconstruction of Stanley House as it might of looked when originally built

out by the architectural evidence; for although the design of the house is "Restoration", the internal panelling which survives is early eighteenth century.

Stanley House originally stood within heavily wooded grounds with tree-lined avenues aligned onto its principal elevations and formal gardens on the north side of the house. To the south there was a walled forecourt with a fine pair of gates and gate piers, aligned onto the front door, which was the main entrance from the King's Road. The stable yard was located to the west of the house.

One unanswered question is whether or not the original house had windows on its east and west elevations. There is no doubt that these elevations did have at least "blind" windows; but the building of the Hamilton Room in the 1820s obliterated the east elevation and only part of the west elevation is still visible today. This has only one window at first floor level and evidence of painted *trompe l'oeil* windows in the other "blind" openings (if present plans for the change of use and conversion of the house are approved, this elevation too will be completely obliterated). Ashdown House on the Berkshire/Oxfordshire borders, built in 1663, has a virtually identical plan to Stanley House and it has windows on all elevations. However, Dr. Alison Maguire who is currently cataloguing the Bodleian Library's Rawlinson Collection of house plans of the 1680s, believes one of these plans to be the Stanley House pattern and that has no windows to the side elevations.

Since Walter Godfrey surveyed the house in 1913, it has undergone several unfortunate alterations and it is today in a poor state of repair. The fine panelled rooms on the first floor are neglected and unused and those on the ground floor which are currently let-out for a variety of social and educational functions, are decorated and furnished in an unsympathetic manner. The future of Stanley House is uncertain…

The architectural and historic importance of Stanley House is such that it demands careful repair and scholarly restoration and that the enjoyment of this particular type of English classical house should be available to the widest possible public. It would certainly be unfortunate if the public were denied even the limited opportunity to enjoy this building which has existed in recent years.

1991

(Note: Stanley House is now in private hands and has been beautifully restored)

St Luke's: Chelsea's Gothic Cathedral

J. Mordaunt Crook

When Charles Eastlake published his *History of the Gothic Revival* in 1872, he chose St. Luke's, Chelsea, as the first true example of the revived Gothic spirit. More than a hundred years later, the date of its building (1819-24) is still regarded by historians as a milestone in architectural history.

Why? Not because of its style: that is a typically Regency mixture of fourteenth, fifteenth and sixteenth-century Gothic. Still less because of its planning: in the original layout of the church there was no hint of ecclesiology or of the Oxford Movement. What made St. Luke's important was its system of construction.

Like most of London, late eighteenth-century Chelsea was expanding fast. By 1801, the parish had grown to 12,000 inhabitants. The original parish church – All Saints, Cheyne Walk; later known as Chelsea Old Church – could accommodate only 450 people. A new church there had to be, and luckily an ideal site was available: the parish burial ground to the north of Kings' Road. In 1806 the decision was taken, but further action was delayed until the end of the Napoleonic War.

St. Luke's, therefore, belongs to that prolific spate of church-building associated with the Church Building Act of 1818. It is not, strictly speaking, a Commissioners' Church: it was only partly paid for by the 1818 Church Commissioners. But in its timing, location and function it epitomises the social and political priorities of Regency Anglicanism. At this date Chelsea was not a rich parish. In fact, for the greater part of the nineteenth century it was an area of poverty and potential disorder. Not for nothing did the Chaplain of Chelsea Hospital, the Reverend Richard Yates, address a famous pamphlet to the Prime Minister, Lord Liverpool, in 1815: *The Church in Danger*. The purpose behind the building of St. Luke's was as much political as philanthropic or spiritual. Parliament had demanded 'fit and proper accommodation for the largest number of persons at the least expense'. Chelsea's new church was to seat 2,000. And on part of the site a new parochial school was to be erected: education, religion and politics in harness. 'Education',

St. Luke's Church

announced the new rector – the Duke of Wellington's brother – in 1826, 'makes useful those members of society who would otherwise be the destruction of it: it makes them good servants, good citizens, good men; above all it instructs them in that holy religion which reconciles them to their station in this present life, and bids them look forward with joy and hope to the everlasting happiness of that which is to come'.

The architect of St. Luke's, James Savage (1779-1852), won the commission in open competition: he defeated John Nash and Sir John Soane. At the time he might well have been chosen in preference to John Rennie as architect of London Bridge. His first design for the tower of St. Luke's – an open masonry lantern in the manner of Wren's St. Dunstan's-in-the-East – was rejected as too adventurous. But he did persuade the Church Commissioners to accept the idea of a full-scale Gothic vault, complete with load-bearing ribs and functional flying buttresses. The result was unique in its day, unequalled indeed until Pugin's time. It was said by contemporaries – and it is still often said – that the roof of St. Luke's was the first masonry Gothic vault to be built in Britain since the Middle Ages. That is certainly not true. Examples of Gothic Survival vaulting can be found in Oxford and the Cotswolds dating from as late as the middle of the eighteenth century. But St. Luke's does boast the first masonry vault of the Gothic Revival, and nothing of that scale – its sixty foot vault matches Wells Cathedral in height – had been built since the early sixteenth century. When the church was consecrated in 1824 the congregation was not surprisingly, rather nervous; it was said they had 'roof on the brain'.

Understandably, the building was expensive. The Coade stone reredos – thought at the time 'to do honour to a cathedral' – was particularly elaborate. But the building process was dogged by incompetence and bad luck. The foundations were flooded while work was in progress. Three successive clerks of works had to be dismissed as inefficient; and the contractor, John Willson, went bankrupt and died. At upwards of £40,000, the church cost more than twice the original estimate. Savage was not a reliable man of business. At St. Luke's, he seems to have exercised inadequate control, and his career came to an unhappy end soon afterwards as a result of his misjudged restoration of the Temple Church. But he did understand Gothic construction, and he appreciated its aesthetic impact. His description of the tower of St. Luke's could hardly be bettered:

"As the building rises, it increases in lightness and decoration…

The character aimed at… has been plainness and stability at the base, lightening gradually as it rises, and finally off against the sky with a feathery lightness and delicacy… Observe a tree, with its massive trunk below, and throwing off the first large branches, and smaller and smaller to the top; which branches, as they extend, become more and more attenuated, until at length the extremities are so delicate as to be moved by the lightest breath of heaven…

Furthermore, this arrangement is peculiarly appropriate for ecclesiastical buildings; and in perfect unison with the general expression of Gothic architecture. The peculiar forms of this style naturally lead the eye upwards; and by a physical necessity the thoughts and the imagination become elevated also."

In other words, the inspirational qualities of Gothic.

Despite minor alterations – to porch and pinnacles outside; to chancel, altar and pulpit inside – Savage's achievement has survived mercifully unscathed. It is to safeguard that achievement – and to restore the eroded masonry of this very remarkable church – that a restoration appeal has been launched.

St. Luke's is a church with more than its fair share of memories. Its first rector – as we have seen – was the Duke of Wellington's brother, Gerald Valerian Wellesley. Another was Gerald Blunt, a significant figure in Oxford Movement liturgy and Christian Socialist philanthropy. Its organists – and the organ is one of the finest in London – have included Thomas Attwood (a pupil of Mozart), Sir John Goss and John Ireland, composer of *Praise my soul the King of Heaven*. There is a fine monument by Chantrey to Lt. Col. Henry Cadogan who fell at the battle of Vittoria in 1813. Other memorials include those of officers killed in the Indian Mutiny and warriors of the Punjab Frontier Force – popularly known as 'Piffers'. Kingsley preached here. Dickens was married here. Carlyle ate mulberries from the rectory garden. St. Luke's is Chelsea's cathedral.

1988

WHAT THEY THOUGHT AT THE TIME

October 1936. The Gropius House

The Times

Of the two houses lately built on the east side of Church Street, "The Times" architectural correspondent wrote last October: –

"Though, or rather because, they are inconspicuous, two recent buildings must be mentioned for their wide implications: the houses opposite the Chelsea Arts Club in Church Street, Chelsea, designed respectively by Professor Walter Gropius and Messrs. Mendelsohn and Chermayeff. In a sense these are the most "advanced" buildings in London, but the odd thing is that they not only tone in with the general character of the neighbourhood, but seem to have a definite relationship to some old, possibly eighteenth century, houses in the same street. It is the nineteenth century that intrudes. The reasons why are well worth pondering, in the presence of the two houses themselves, by anybody who is concerned about neighbourliness in contemporary architecture."

The Gropius House

For the further education of our less "advanced" members the verdict of the same authority upon the new Emporium at Sloane Square may be quoted: –

"A building which gives so much pleasure and entertainment as to make one feel that there must be a catch in it somewhere, is the new Peter Jones at the corner of King's Road, Sloane Square. It is, in effect, a glass cage, rounding into the Square on a double curve, the ground floor affording an uninterrupted display, under cover, against a cyclorama back-ground. This building, designed by Messrs. Slater & Moberly, with professor C. H. Reilly as associated architect, vindicates a principle of construction in a way that can only be called revolutionary.

When shops began to open out their ground floors for window display, a common criticism was that the building above looked insufficiently supported. Paradoxical as it may sound, the real reason for this was that stylistic requirements kept up the pretence that external walls had still a supporting function. At Peter Jones the bluff is called; and with practically no visible supports on the ground floor, the building looks perfectly stable, because the mushroom construction, cantilevered out to the canopy, declares itself at a glance – a striking illustration, free from moral taint, of the practical advantages of truth over prevarication."

This frankly expressed modernist view of Chelsea's latest architectural acquisitions must be left to the acceptance or rejection of our members; but without throwing stones at Peter Jones' "glass cage" it may be pointed out that for all its glassiness the ground floor is entirely dependent upon artificial light; and that, to many of us, the look of stability in the mushroom construction of the cantilevered front is by no means obvious.

At poker, "bluff" has been defined as an imposition: at Sloane Square its calling suggests for many of us something of an imposture. If we must have "glass cages", they should surely at least give their inmates daylight.

1936

'MIGHTY SWELLS DWELL HERE'

The Makers of Tite Street

Alice Berkeley

"Alongside the artistic squalour [of workingman's Chelsea] we have the curious contrast of artistic splendour in a blazing brand-new quarter, of which the sacred centre is Tite Street, " wrote Benjamin Ellis Martin in *Old Chelsea* in 1899. "Here amid much that is good and genuine in our modern manner, there is an aggressive affectation of antiquity shown by the little houses and studios obtruding on the street, by the grandiose piles of mansions towering on the embankment: all in raging red brick, and in the so-called Queen Anne style… mighty swells dwell here, and here pose some famous farceurs in art and literature."

One hundred and sixty-eight years before Tite Street was laid out, the third Earl of Carberry, Lord Vaughan, built a large country house on Paradise Row (now Cheyne Place and Royal Hospital Road) in Chelsea with formal gardens sweeping down to the Thames. While he was Governor General of Jamaica he had recouped his family fortune through devious business dealings and exploitation of his staff, aided and abetted by the piratical Henry Morgan, his Lieutenant Governor. His new country estate adjoined the row of grand houses which lined the river between the Royal Hospital and Lindsey House. Gough House, as it came to be known under his successors, was built about 1707 in the most up-to-date style, with steps leading to raised ground-floor reception rooms and with high windows to lighten the interior and afford excellent views of the garden and river. Although he was appointed a Lord Commissioner of the Admiralty, Lord Vaughan was shunned by society because of his disreputable friends, and Pepys called him "one of the lewdest fellows of the age." He abandoned his monstrously ugly wife, Lady Anne, at the altar, so never produced a legitimate heir.

Lord Vaughan died in his carriage on the road to Chelsea in 1713 and the house was sold to the Gough family, merchants in the India and China trade who were "good worthy folk, happy in having no history." After the last male heir, Thomas Pemberton, died in 1790 his wife started an Establishment for Education of Young Ladies in the house, and it appears that the school continued to operate until its transformation to the Victoria Hospital for Children in 1866.

In the 1870s, the Metropolitan Board of Works supervised the construction of the Embankment along the Thames, and apparently forced the compulsory purchase of a strip of land beside the river to obtain the space it needed to build the highway and to run sewers parallel to the river – following which the land was leased for development. East of Swan Walk and skirting the grounds of the Victoria Hospital for Children, plots were laid out on either side of a short street named in 1875 for Sir William Tite, a former Chairman of the Board of Works.

Whistler led the band of artists, writers, actresses and society ladies who came to live in Tite Street, and his friend E. W. Godwin, who Max Beerbohm dubbed, "the greatest aesthete of them all," built large airy studios in which they pursued beauty and taste in the best natural light. The first to arrive in 1877, Whistler leased a double plot just in from the Embankment for £29 per annum, with the strict proviso that all building plans had to be approved by the Board of Works. He and Godwin collaborated on plans for a house which would reflect Adam simplicity with an asymmetrical oriental flavour. Permission to build was refused until Victorian decorations were added around the windows and over the front door. Whistler promised to put a statue in the niche over the front door; it was ordered but never arrived. The White House was built with two studios, with the thought that one could be used as an atelier for paying students. Unfortunately there was no time to put this practical plan into action before Whistler's bankruptcy sale ended his stay there. In 1879 the house was sold to Harry Quilter for £2,700. How unnerving for poor Whistler to have to make way for this stocky, brash, short-tempered amateur painter who wielded great power as art critic for *The Times* of London.

Once Whistler had moved into the White House, Godwin drew up plans for a studio for Frank Miles (No.44), whose pastel portraits of society beauties brought him great social and financial success. He was anxious to move into Whistler's orbit, and brought with him to share the house a young friend called Oscar Wilde. Both Whistler and Miles enjoyed promoting him as a fellow aesthete. Even though Godwin had to make changes to satisfy the Board of Works, Keats House, as Wilde called it, was one of his most successful buildings, with the spare oriental influence visible

Oscar Wilde, circa 1898

both inside and out; his delicate staircase and panelled rooms are unchanged today. Laura Troubridge, who was to move to Tite Street after her marriage, was invited to tea at Keats House and wrote in her diary, "June 30th, 1879. To tea with Tardy (Orde), met Oscar Wilde, the poet. Both fell awfully in love with him, thought him quite delightful." In July she and Tardy went again, "great fun, lots of vague 'intense' men, such duffers, who amused us awfully. The room was a mass of white lilies, photos of Mrs. Langtry, peacock-feather screens and coloured pots, pictures of various merit."

Oscar left Keats House to go to America, and when Frank Miles went mad in 1887 and was sent to an asylum, it was sold to the Misses Dixon. Five years later the court painter Percy Jacomb-Hood bought it and lived there for more than thirty years. In later life he married a noble Dutch lady who wore a red wig and adored small boys.

Godwin's next Tite Street project was a double studio opposite the White House for two painter friends: Archie Stuart-Wortley and Charles Pellegrini, creator of the "Spy" cartoons. They parted company within a year and Stuart-Wortley sold the house in 1879 to Slingsby Bethell, who named it Chelsea Lodge. Another owner, the American Edwin Austin Abbey, R.I., proposed turning the house into a museum for the Royal Academy, but his death and the First World War interfered with this plan and the house was torn down between the wars to make way for the present block of flats.

Next door to Chelsea Lodge was the controversial Shelley Theatre, built by Sir Percy Shelley, son of the poet and Mary Wollstonecraft. He and his architect Joseph Peacock were founding members of the Queen Anne revival; they had built Shelley House at 1 Chelsea Embankment in 1876. Three years later he asked the Metropolitan Board of Works if he could take a lease on a large plot next to Chelsea Lodge in Tite Street. The lease included a covenant prohibiting the construction of a theatre, music hall, or any place of entertainment. Shelley signed it in May, 1879, then immediately commissioned Joseph Peacock to design a private theatre behind an anonymous Queen Anne style red brick exterior. The first play was performed there in 1881, and performances for the Shelleys and their friends, or for charity benefits, continued to be given regularly for the next year. They were advertised in a theatrical paper and reviewed in the national press, and in December 1882 it was announced in the *Morning Post* that the Prince and Princess of Wales and other members of the Royal Family would attend the opening of the newest play. The evening was deemed "a dramatic and social triumph". Next door, at Chelsea Lodge, the Hon. Slingsby Bethell was not amused. He instructed his solicitor to draw the attention of the Board of Works to this blatant transgression of the terms of Shelley's covenant. Even when prosecution proceedings against him had started, Shelley produced a play to benefit the Victoria Hospital. Finally the full force of the law was brought to bear, he was fined one shilling and the theatre closed. The buildings, which stood empty for many years, was eventually bought and pulled down by Sir Charles Oppenheimer. Shelley Court, the block of flats at 56 Tite Street, was built in 1899.

In 1876, shortly after Godwin ended a long affair with England's greatest actress Ellen Terry, he married Beatrice, the very young daughter of the sculptor John Bernie Phillips, who had come down from Glasgow to work on the Albert Memorial. Presumably Godwin convinced Phillips to build Dhu House next door to the Shelley Theatre in 1881. After Godwin died, Beatrice married Whistler and moved to Whistler's studio a few doors away, taking her trousseau which consisted of "a new toothbrush and a new sponge." Two of her sisters continued to live in Dhu House (No.54) until they both were almost 100 years old. Over the years they collected hundreds of Whistler's works, which finally were left to Glasgow University.

More House (No.52), was built in 1882 by the architect Frederick Waller for the Hon. John Collier, his brother-in-law. Collier's studio was airy and elegant, but reached by a rather steep and angular staircase which made it impossible to move large pictures out of the house. Eventually a trap door was cut into the studio floor so that canvases lowered through it could slide directly out of the side door.

After his wife's death, Collier fell in love with her younger sister. As it was then illegal to marry one's deceased wife's sister, they ran away to be married in Norway and lived there for about a year. After returning to More House they were snubbed by Collier's older brother, who lived around the corner on the Embankment, and forced to move to St. John's Wood, "where it didn't matter what you did," says Felix Hope-Nicholson, "and I believe still doesn't."

Laura and Adrian Hope bought More House in 1892. Their grandson, Felix Hope-Nicholson, lives there today and retells many stories of life in Tite Street. The house has changed very little since the turn of the century except, perhaps, for staff arrangements. "My grandmother had eight servants, and I often wonder where they slept – I think largely with each other. There was no heating upstairs, it was very cold, and I think they were frightened of the dark."

Opposite More House were The Studios (No.33) and a large studio house (No.31) both built by R. W. Edis in 1880. Well-known artists have always lived there, of whom John Singer Sargent was probably the most prominent. Although he had a large studio in the Fulham Road, he took a lease on one of The Studios in 1885 in order to be able to receive his sitters in more elegant surroundings. Six years later he expanded into even grander quarters net door, a "beautiful, high, cool studio," wrote Henry James, "opening upon a balcony that overhangs a charming Chelsea green garden, adding a charm to everything." Max Beerbohm painted an amusing sketch of duchesses lined up outside No.31 waiting to have their portraits painted.

"My grandmother knew Sargent well, " recounts Felix Hope-Nicholson, "and he said to her once, 'I can't go in or out of my house without seeing a child go in or out of yours.' My grandmother especially went in for painting portraits of children. Sargent said he simply hated painting children. He felt very sorry for my grandmother."

Next door to Sargent's establishment was Canwell House (No. 29), which Stuart-Wortley had also commissioned from Godwin in 1879. A succession of artists including an American Miss Bigelow, the sculptress Miss Mary Grant, and Percy Bigland lived there before it became the Princess Mary Nursing Home for the Victoria Hospital. Sadly the house was pulled down at the same time as the hospital in the 1960s.

The Cottage (No.50), was built in 1882 for the painter Anna Lea Merritt, one of several American ladies who have enjoyed the slightly bohemian grandeur of Tite Street. She had the distinction of being the first lady artist to sell a painting to the Tate Gallery, and *Love Locked Out* still hangs there. Her lease was taken over by Percy Bigland, who seemed to hop back and forth across the street from one studio to the other.

The Tower House (No.46), is the one building on Tite Street which is pure Godwin design, unadulterated by the opinions and taste of the members of the Board of Works. In 1878, Mrs. Eleanor Bagot, an admiral's widow, leased the site next to The Cottage and asked Godwin to draw plans for a block of studios which she could build for investment. The first plans were rejected, but by December, 1883, Mrs. Bagot had contrived to buy the freehold, and in 1885, the year before Godwin's death, the Tower House was up. It is said that for several years it was the tallest building in Chelsea; without doubt it was the boldest architecturally, with its stark exterior only relieved by asymmetrical windows. The studios at No.48 were added in the 1890s on the space which remained in Mrs. Bagot's plot.

Oscar Wilde had left Keats House in 1881 to go on his lecture tour of America. He came back two years later with enough money to take a lease a few doors to the north (No.34) in a row of speculative housing built by the architect Frederick Beeston and his relative Francis Butler. Wilde asked Godwin to decorate the interior, which the architect did with panache, but not in haste. The bright white front door and entrance hall led into a shadowy blue and gold Moorish library. In the dark green drawing room on the first floor Whistler had painted golden dragons on the ceiling and later replaced them with Japanese feathers inserted into the plaster. The front drawing room was painted flesh pink with gold cornices surrounding the ceiling covered in Japanese leather. Wilde's study was white, with a yellow ceiling and red lacquer woodwork. These aesthetic heights in interior decoration were not accomplished without several changes of builders and a law suit, but finally the bills were paid and Oscar and his wife Constance moved into their splendid house in January, 1885. They spent ten apparently happy years there; Wilde wrote *The Importance of Being Ernest* and *Lady Windermere's Fan*, and they produced two children. By the time they became neighbours, Laura Hope had become sadly disenchanted with Wilde, "He is grown enormously fat, with a huge face and tight curls all over his head – not at all the aesthetic he used to look," and the first time they met she found Constance "shy and dull". In the long run, however, they did become friends and after Oscar's scandalous trial and imprisonment, Adrian Hope was appointed guardian to the Wildes' sons.

Ellen Terry, on the other hand, thought, "the most remarkable men I have known were Whistler and Oscar Wilde... both of them more instantaneously individual and audacious than it is possible to describe." She and her co-star Henry Irving frequently dined with the Wildes, and she often came to Tite Street during the day to be painted, sculpted or etched in one studio or another. Wilde was at the window the day she passed his house on her way to pose in costume for Sargent, and he reflected, "The street that on a wet and dreary morning has vouchsafed the vision of Lady Macbeth in full regalia magnificently seated in a four-wheeler can never again be as other streets: it must always be full of wonderful possibilities."

1988

LILLIE LANGTRY 1853–1929

Jane Dorrell

Beautiful, ambitious, charming and hard-working, Lillie de Breton was the daughter of the Dean of Jersey where she grew up. In 1874 she married an Irishman, Edward Langtry, more it would seem for his yacht than for love. As soon as they came to London she was a *succès fou*: painted by Millais – as 'The Jersey Lily' which was to be her soubriquet – and by Burne-Jones, Watts and Lord Leighton. She met Rossetti, Swinburne and Oscar Wilde. Soon news of her beauty spread and people would stand on chairs the better to see her when she rode in Rotten Row. She soon caught the roving eye of the Prince of Wales who was to be her lover and friend until his death. His friendship survived her affair with his nephew Prince Louis of Battenberg whose daughter she bore but whom she was unable to marry because her neglected husband refused to divorce her. (The child was brought up by her grandmother in Jersey). Mr Langtry was made bankrupt in 1881 and nothing more is heard of him until 1897 when Lillie was finally granted a divorce in California and he, poor man, came to an untimely end under a train at Crewe.

But in 1881 Mrs Langtry was thinking about her future. A friend suggested the stage, and she 'tried out' at, of all unlikely places, Twickenham Town Hall. There followed a charity matinée at the Haymarket, a season with the Bancrofts, and her career was launched. She spent the next 35 years touring in Britain and America with financial backing from 'admirers'.

When she sailed into New York in 1882 she was rapturously received – then as now Americans loved a royal scandal. Wilde, there to greet her, said to reporters: "I would rather have discovered Mrs Langtry than discovered America". She did not return the compliment. Thirteen years later when her old friend was in the dock rather than on it she was not among those who remained loyal to him.

Lillie Langtry by Frank Miles

In 1889 she moved into 21 Pont Street which was her London home for eight years. When she left the house was taken over by the Cadogan Hotel and today the Langtry rooms are hired out for private parties. In 1899 she married a baronet, Hugo de Bathe but this did not stop her frequenting the gaming-tables of Monte Carlo with a certain Baron Renshaw (aka Edward VII). The king also shared her interest in horse-racing and they owned neighbouring stables in Newmarket. She retired from the theatre in 1917 and after the war bought a villa in Monaco where she died. She wrote her memoirs "The Days I Knew" in 1921. She was not quite so lily-white as she was made out to be.

1996

WALTER GREAVES

Tom Pocock

It is one of the great views of the world. James McNeill Whistler might have called it an arrangement in sky, brick and water. It is taken for granted, but Whistler's Reach of the Thames at Chelsea, ranks beside the Seine in Paris, the lagoon of Venice and the Golden Horn of Istanbul. It has changed little since Whistler painted its moods, "when the evening mist clothes the riverside with poetry as with a veil, and the poor buildings lose themselves in the dim sky and the tall chimneys become campanili and the warehouses are palaces in the night and the whole city hangs in the heavens before us...."

But it may not survive. The West Cross Route is due to span the Thames where the lights of Cremorne rippled on the water, and the shingle beach below Whistler's studio window on Cheyne Walk, where the houseboats now lie, is to become a motorway. When this is done, the lost beauty will be preserved in the paintings of Whistler and of Walter Greaves.

It is appropriate that they should share this. The story of Whistler and Greaves is the stuff of legends. Like all great legends it has mystery and symbolism and strikes an echo from universal experience. It is a story of friendship.

Walter Greaves was, like the Chelsea where he was born in 1846, simple, robust and almost rustic. Like Chelsea, he had sophistication thrust upon him. Like Chelsea, he emerged with those fresh and original qualities that gave so distinct an individuality to the place besieged by the grey metropolis.

Early Victorian Chelsea, although in the process of being joined to London by Belgravia and South Kensington, was a vigorous little country town with river and road transport and market gardening as its principal occupations. Walter Greaves's father, Charles, was a waterman and boat-builder, living in what is now 104 Cheyne Walk with his boats and pontoons moored on the shingle below the river wall. Artists and writers had begun to settle in Chelsea. Turner, incognito, had taken a cottage nearby and Charles Greaves would row him across to Battersea when a splendid sunset was expected.

When the night sky was wild with cloud and moonlight, the Greaves boys would be sent to wake another artist neighbour John Martin, who would bustle out on to his balcony to sketch designs for huge, apocalyptic paintings of Judgement Day. Carlyle had settled in Cheyne Row and Rossetti and the Pre-Raphaelites were to follow.

Walter and his brother Henry were apprenticed in their father's boatyard and one of their duties was to paint heraldic designs on the City's ceremonial barges which were berthed at Chelsea. They took to sketching Chelsea streets and Walter said later that when only sixteen he had painted a large canvas in oils, *Hammersmith Bridge on Boat Race Day*, a masterpiece of primitive art, which now hangs in the Tate Gallery.

Exactly when he painted this picture and exactly when he met young Jimmy Whistler is not certain and the story of Walter Greaves is given an air of mystery by the difficulty of connecting events with dates. Partly this is because much of the story emerged when Greaves was old and his memory weak, and partly because, among the many Whistlerian mannerisms he was to adopt, was a deliberate superstition about being committed to definite times and places. Therefore, it is not known when Greaves and Whistler first met. Greaves said that it was in the late 1850's but Whistler did not come to live at what is now 101 Cheyne Walk, until 1863.

Aged twenty-nine, Jimmy Whistler was a brilliant, dashing young American painter, trained in the Paris of Trilby and the early Impressionists. He had been staying with his sister and her husband, Seymour Haden, the amateur etcher, at 62 Sloane Street, but had fled from the upper middle-class formalities of their household to create his own bohemian world which he was to bequeath to Chelsea. At this time, his neighbours, the Greaves family, were ideal companions. There was a pretty daughter, Alice – nicknamed 'Tinnie' – to flirt with and squire to dances at Cremorne pleasure gardens down the road. There were the boys to take him rowing on the Thames and on explorations of the jumble of old inns, warehouses and wharves that rambled down to the water on either side of Chelsea Old Church.

There was fair exchange in the friendship between Whistler and Walter Greaves. Whistler taught Walter to paint in what was then a revolutionary style and the puzzled Greaves boys complained that whereas, to them, a boat was always a boat, to Jimmy Whistler it was a tone. Walter taught Jimmy to handle a boat with such success that Whistler had a sailor suit made for rowing expeditions, which sometimes lasted all night and ranged as far as Putney.

Later, these seemed idyllic years. Whistler, under the influence of Japanese art, had begun to paint his lovely, mysterious nocturnes – or, as he first called them, 'moonlights '– of the river. On the Thames with Walter or Henry at the oars, he would memorise a view-sometimes buildings with lighted windows against a pale sky, sometimes the lights of Cremorne – and make notes with white chalk on brown paper and commit the subject to canvas in his studio next morning. Cremorne, with its lights, fireworks and multi-coloured dresses, fascinated Whistler. "We used to row down the river opposite the gardens," recalled Walter, "when he loved to pick the pinks, blues and other colours out amongst the lights."

Walter Greaves also began to paint nocturnes in oils under Whistler's tuition and, it was then thought, in straight imitation. But, as a critic of *The Times* wrote years later, "Whistler himself was

A self-portrait by Walter Greaves, circa 1970

happiest in evasion, while Greaves was by nature explicit, and, moreover, his art was positively inspired by the subject interest that Whistler thought unimportant." At about this time, Whistler painted *Old Battersea Bridge*: *Nocturne in Blue and Gold*, which now hangs in the Tate, and Greaves painted his nocturne, *Passing Under Battersea Bridge*. Because, half a century later, Walter could not, or would not, remember exactly when he painted this, the consequences were to be disastrous.

The friendship between Greaves and Whistler lasted some twenty years. But, gradually, the first, fresh gaiety and intimacy lessened, and Walter became not so much a companion and confidant as unpaid studio assistant and, sometimes, servant. Jimmy Whistler was ascending socially, mixing with the intellectuals, who were drifting down to Chelsea, and the smart sets of Kensington and Mayfair. But, while his need for the undemanding friendship of the Greaves family lessened, Whistler remained Walter's hero. In dress and mannerism, as well as in painting, Greaves adoringly followed 'The Master's' lead. Against his father's advice, he had given up his boat-yard trade and thought of himself as a professional artist, proudly signing his work 'A Pupil of Whistler'.

The rejection of Walter Greaves by Whistler was final and shattering. After the libel action against Ruskin in 1878 had brought bankruptcy and the loss of the White House, which he had built in Tite Street, Whistler exiled himself to Venice and when he returned he no longer regarded Walter as a friend. He had discarded his mistresses and married, was enjoying more challenging company in his studio and had matched wits with Oscar Wilde. Perhaps he was irritated by the unquestioning adoration of Greaves and with himself for responding to it. Probably he was even more irritated when his humble pupil expressed ideas of his own and spoke of painting up to the standard of the Royal Academy. And certainly the first legal Mrs. Whistler was averse to any reminders of her husband's bohemian past.

Greaves, later, would only say that after Whistler married he had 'vanished', adding wistfully, "I went mad over Whistler. I can see him now with his scowl and his top hat over his eyes.... He was a very nice fellow... but he wanted knowing."

Knowing Whistler's moods, Greaves always hoped that they would change and their friendship be resumed. It never happened. His humble approaches were brutally and publicly snubbed and, in 1903, when Whistler was dying, Greaves called at the house only to be turned away at the door. There is a sketch by Walter of Whistler's funeral procession at the door of Chelsea Old Church-but it was drawn from the far side of the road.

Perhaps reasons for Whistler's behaviour were in a bundle of 'very personal letters' which Greaves showed to a friend in later years. Knowing Greaves to be in extreme poverty and near starvation, the friend remarked that they were 'worth a fortune', at which Walter at once tore them up and threw them on the fire, saying, "They were private letters. Now I can never be tempted to destroy that privacy." These were hard years for Greaves, his pictures did not sell and he was reduced to hawking his drawings at half-a-crown a piece in the streets. "Walter Greaves was quite a sad affair, " recalls a Chelsean who remembers him. "He seemed to lead a very lonely life. There was nothing cheerful about him."

Fame came unexpectedly and with devastating suddenness. In 1911, William Marchant, proprietor of the fashionable Goupil Gallery, discovered a mass of Greaves's paintings, drawings and etchings in a second-hand bookshop, had them cleaned and put on exhibition. It was a sensational success. Critics not only hailed him as 'An Unknown Master' and reported 'Discovery of a Great Artist' and 'Mr. Walter Greaves's Leap to Fame'; some actually declared that he was a greater painter than Whistler. The *Daily Mail* critic had noticed that Greaves's nocturne of Old Battersea Bridge was dated 1862 and wrote that, as Whistler's somewhat similar nocturne had been painted ten years later, this proved that it had been Greaves who inspired Whistler and not vice versa. This was too much for friends of the dead Whistler. They discovered that Greaves had signed and dated his picture just before the exhibition opened. They claimed, moreover, that many of the works on exhibition were not by Greaves at all but were discarded Whistlers, stolen, touched up and signed by his former pupil.

Fame had lasted a fortnight when the storm broke. Walter Sickert and other painters rushed to Greaves's defence, but the scandal was too exciting to be stopped. Bewildered and protesting his innocence, Walter Greaves faded again into obscurity and poverty. But his tragedy remained in the memories of other artists and, after the First World War, a group of them sought him out and set about restoring his reputation. This was done by men such as William Nicholson, William Rothenstein, Walter Sickert, Max Beerbohm and Augustus John. A dinner was given for Walter Greaves at the Chelsea Arts Club and he was elected an honorary member. He was now over seventy, and a place was found for him as a Poor Brother at Charterhouse, where he died in 1930.

L-R: William Nicholson, Walter Greaves, Augustus John and William Merchant

Since then, Walter Greaves' work has been increasingly recognised as his own achievement and a unique, though sometimes muddled, contribution to English painting. There are his oils, some Whistlerian but with a decisive quality of their own, others showing only the work of a highly individual Greaves. There are drawings of Chelsea, intricately-detailed street scenes with a curiously haunted look and the sometimes crude sketches that the artist hawked in the streets. And lovely, delicate etchings that some consider his finest work. About them all is what Sickert described as 'a rare intensity and passion'.

Jimmy Whistler lies near the river, beneath a noble bronze monument at Chiswick. Walter Greaves lies among the old men of Charterhouse beneath a small institutional headstone in the churchyard at Little Hallingbury in Essex. But their memorial is also at Chelsea. It happens each evening soon after the sun sets over the river. As twilight falls, the shapes of barges, wharves and warehouses are thrown into strong relief; the tide flows and this is the river of Walter Greaves. Then the light lessens and blurs and boats become tones, lights reflections and the poor buildings lose themselves in the dim sky. This is the river of Whistler. But for a few moments in the fading of the light it belongs to them both.

1967

WHISTLER IN TITE STREET

Harry Waldron Havemeyer

In September 1881, Louisine Waldron Elder called on J. McNeill Whistler at his studio, No.13 Tite Street in Chelsea, for the purpose of meeting the artist and looking at some of his work. She acquired on that visit five of his Venice pastels on brown paper for £30, all that she had to spend of her pocket money. She later gave the five pastels to her friend, Charles L. Freer. Today they are in the Freer Gallery of Art, Smithsonian Institution, Washington DC.

In 1888, the numbering of Tite Street was changed. The studio building No.13 became No.33 and remains so today. This building was designed by R.W. Edis as studios for artists and was completed early in 1881. Whistler moved in upon his return from Venice in May that year The building stood directly north of the famous White House (No.15 now 35 Tite Street) designed for Whistler by E W. Godwin, the notable architect, and built between October 1877 and the fall of 1878. Whistler had barely settled into his White House that fall when the Ruskin libel case blew up.

John Ruskin, the famous art critic, had commented about Whistler's paintings, *Nocturne in Black and Gold: the Falling Rocket* (Tate Gallery London), "I never expected to hear a coxcomb ask 200 guineas for flinging a pot of paint in the public's face." Whistler, furious at the remark, sued Ruskin for libel. Although he won his suit, he was awarded only a farthing in damages and the White House had to be sold to pay his legal costs. Whistler was declared bankrupt and moved to Venice for a year. It was upon his return that he moved into No.13 Tite Street.

He remained in that location until 1885 when he was followed there by John Sargent. In 1901, Sargent acquired the Edis-designed house next door to the north (No.11 now 31 Tite Street) where the commemorative carving is seen today This house had been built for Frank Dicey, a portrait painter and member of Whistler's circle of artists.

Thirty-three Tite Street, known as The Studios, has been occupied by a number of artists over the years. In addition to Whistler and Sargent, the portraitist, Augustus John worked and lived there.

Today it is the studio and home of landscape artist, Julian Barrow and his family. In March 1985, Louisine Elder's grandson, Harry Waldron Havemeyer called on Julian Barrow to see some of his work in the same building as his grandmother did 103 years before. He acquired two of Barrow's works for his London home, one for £175, the other for £225.

Sadly, Whistler's White House next door, where he barely lived at all, was demolished in the 1960s to be replaced by an ugly modern structure. Otherwise, Tite Street appears today much as it must have looked to Louisine Elder in 1881.

From *Sixteen to Sixty, Memoirs of a Collector*,
Louisine W. Havemeyer

My acquaintance with Whistler, not with his works but with Whistler himself, began when I was a girl in my teens. I think it was the year after I bought my first Monet and my first Degas. I was passing the season in London with my mother and a friend of hers, and we visited an exhibition in Grafton Street. It was the first time I saw Whistler's work, and I cannot at this moment recall all the portraits or 'Nocturne' he exhibited there, but I know I was deeply impressed with the portrait of 'Little Miss Alexander' which I believe was shown there for the first time. At any rate the portrait created a furore with the public and with the critics and also with me. The critics led the public like the poor *tête de mouton* that it is, and one could hear in the gallery passing from picture to picture its silly remarks based upon the morning criticisms in the leading dailies.

The fascination of the little Alexander girl's portrait appealed to me very much: the movement, the color, and the originality of the composition interested me and almost involuntarily I remarked: "I wish I could have an example of Whistler's work. Do you suppose it would do any good to write to him?" I addressed my remark to my mother's friend. Smilingly, she answered: "We can try, " and we did, with the result that we presented ourselves a few days later at the White House in Cheyne Walk and were immediately admitted into a room I shall never forget.

Although we sat down, I do not recall any furniture in the room, not even chairs; I was so impressed with the lovely yellow light that seemed to envelop us and which began right at the floor and mounted to the ceiling in the most harmonious gradations until you felt you were sitting in the soft glow of a June sunset. Two objects in the room arrested the eye: near the window stood a blue and white hawthorn jar which held one or two sprays of long reedy grass, and in the center of the room there was a huge Japanese bronze vase; it loomed up in that mellow light with the solemnity of an altar and might have been dedicated to the lares and penates of the household. It seemed to me no Grecian home could have been more beautiful or more classic. I have since been many times in Whistler's renowned Peacock Room, but I assure you it impressed me far less than this one did when I was ushered into it on that May afternoon.

"Jimmy Whistler"

Whistler entered almost immediately. Instantly I felt a flash as I looked at him and an impression was printed forever indelibly upon my memory. I gave a second glance and I was persuaded that Whistler had made that room as a background for himself. He was a black Loge against the yellow light. I cannot think of him otherwise, Loge the fire god, restless, excitable, with a burning intelligence concentrated in his piercing black eyes, a personality with a power to focus itself beyond resistance, a power that enjoyed the shock it produced, and a gay spontaneous irrelevance. He certainly was a Loge incarnate, a fire who emitted the sparks he swallowed and laughed as the shower fell upon the public whom he held in such contempt. I assure you I was thrilled as I shook his hand and felt at once that I could anticipate a new experience. Strange to say I immediately was at ease and had no fear of him. 1 made a direct statement of my errand. I said: "I have thirty pounds to spend and, Mr. Whistler, Oh indeed I should like something of yours. Have you anything you would like me to have?"

He stood still just a second and looked at me, and I looked at the white lock in his intensely black hair. "Why do you want something of mine?" he asked

"Because I have seen your exhibition and – because Miss Cassatt likes your etchings, " I answered.

"Do you know Miss Cassatt?" he asked quickly.

"Indeed I do, " I answered. "She is my best friend, and I owe it to her that I have a Pissaro, a Monet, and a Degas

"You have a Degas?" he asked looking at me curiously "Yes," I said, "I bought it last year with my spending money. It is a beautiful ballet scene and cost me five hundred francs," I added earnestly, for I have always wanted price understood, "I have just thirty pounds – that's all I can spend, so please tell me if it is impossible."

"No, it is not impossible," he answered kindly, "let us go into the studio and I will see what I have," and he led the way into the studio, which I don't need to describe as everyone knows what a studio is like, with its easels and hangings, the enormous windows and spooky lay figures and messy old stuffs and its many portfolios.

Whistler went directly to one of the portfolios, and when we were seated he began taking out the pastels he had done in Venice when he was there and had brought back with him to use as notes in making his Venetian set of etchings; pastels of doorways, of bridges, of "Nocturnes", of churches, of anything he could use when he returned to London and did the set of etchings that has become so famous. I sometimes wonder if he ever knew that Mr. Havemeyer

bought the original set which was exhibited in the white and gold room, and in white and gold frames. I wonder if perhaps his dealer told him, or perhaps Charles L. Freer, who knows? I had to exclaim, "how fine" as he drew out a pastel of a doorway.

"You like that?" he asked, so quickly that again I thought he was Loge.

"Oh, so much, " I answered. "You have done so little and yet it is just Venice as I remember it."

Whistler placed it against the portfolio, and taking out another he said: "Don't you like that brown paper as a background? It has a value, hasn't it? But it sets the critics by the ears, you know they

Portrait of Whistler by Walter Greaves

think I'm mad." He gave a little laugh and took out another pastel and I saw by his expression that it recalled something to him. He continued: "Do you know the critics hate me so they are using themselves up trying to get back at me?" Whistler finally selected five pastels for me. I put them in a row upon the floor and knelt down to admire them. I fumbled in my pocket until I found my pound notes and I deliberately shook them out and handed them to him saying:

"Are you not ashamed to compare them with these?" And I gave a proud wave over my lovely pastels.

Whistler appeared to be amused at my disdain of his mercenary instincts. He told me he had done those five in Venice and did not expect to sell them. "I call that 'Nocturne,'" he said, pointing to the brown paper background on which there was a bridge over a lagoon, "do you like the name?" It was Venice enveloped in the beautiful mystery of night.

"It is just the title for it," I acquiesced. "I have been there myself, have stood upon that bridge and have felt just what I guess you felt. Do you know that lovely American word? I got it from our Yankee dialect." I was ashamed I had said "guess" but I feared Whistler might think me sentimental. "I guess I do, "answered Whistler, lightly falling into the dialect himself, "and I guess I'd better put the title of each pastel on the back of its frame, and you can tell them 'over there' what they mean."

I remember that Oscar Wilde and a friend came in and that Whistler served us a cup of tea very deftly and very daintily. I wondered how he managed to do it, and he joked all the time with Oscar Wilde, who it seemed to me was quite equal to Whistler in repartee, but not in the knowledge of art. I asked Whistler, when he appeared quite comfortable and happy after one or two cups of tea, to tell us about his art. Of course I did not put it just that way, but said something about the "Little Miss Alexander" portrait that, I think, pleased him, for he began talking about his methods and his inspirations. It was another Whistler, quite firm, quite earnest. For the first time I heard of the harmony of the palette. "Even when you begin," he said, "the portrait must be upon your palette and beware how you change it, or you will have to take another canvas and begin all over again." I remember how quietly we sat, how eagerly we listened; it was a golden memory. For at least an hour he spoke eloquently and earnestly about his profession.

These memoirs, if wanting in literary merit, are at least strictly truthful, and after so many years – more than a generation has elapsed since that afternoon – it is still vividly bright in my memory, and although I do not dare try to repeat all Whistler said, I know to this day I break a lance in his defense when anyone accuses him of flippancy or insincerity in regard to his art. He may have played to the gallery, because, forsooth, he understood *coeur et âme* the British public. He loved to be Loge to his critics and to see them sizzle and squirm as he showered the sparks of his witticisms about them, but to his muse his attitude was ever dignified and noble and respectful. Like every mortal he had his limitations, and where he failed it was an honest failure, where he succeeded success was the result of an equally honest effort. There was much light and shade in the life of Whistler, both as artist and as man.

One evening in our hotel in Jermyn Street my mother became restless and said she would sit up no longer for Whistler's promised visit. It was after eleven o'clock, and I was still begging my mother's friend to wait 'just a little longer" when Whistler was announced, and as gaily and cheerily as any troubadour he walked in and greeted us, with his wand in one hand and the bundle of pastels in the other. He appeared unconscious that the hour was late. He had evidently enjoyed a good dinner at his club or an amusing piece at some theatre, for he was in a merry mood and entertained us for an hour or two. He showed me the pastels and he called my attention to the frames. "You see," he said, "the frame is a very important matter and I had to have the gold changed several times before I was satisfied. I have also had the title of each pastel put on the back and added the 'butterfly'. You know my signature of course?" he added, "but you don't know about the sting," and he explained that at times he signed the butterfly with the sting and at others without it, but always for reasons best known to himself – and the critics.

Again lest my memory betray me, I do not dare to try to repeat all that he said that evening, but I know that he touched upon every subject of interest in London at the time, artistic, theatrical, and literary; and only when I knew it was fast approaching two o'clock and I felt I owed something to my mother and her friend, I frankly said:

"Mr. Whistler, I think it is time for you to go." He did not take it at all amiss but said naively: "Is it late?" and as I laughed at him he rather made an apology for his bad habit of turning night into day, and bade us goodnight. I never saw him again.

Written circa 1920 and republished in 2002 by The Chelsea Society

VERONESE IN FULHAM ROAD

Anybody who has walked through the halls and corridors, or sat in the waiting-rooms, of the Chelsea and Westminster Hospital will be aware of its use of art as therapy. The hospital's Arts Project has, under distinguished patronage, made practical and effective use of the visual arts to cheer and comfort those for whom it offers medical support. But anybody who happens to enter its little chapel will see something even more extraordinary. This is the dreamlike experience of entering a church in Venice to be dazzled by a great Venetian painting.

The painting above the altar is indeed by the sixteenth century Venetian master Veronese. His name was, in fact, Paolo Caliari but he was called Veronese because he had been born in Verona although it is to the Venetian School that his work belongs. This is one of six paintings for altar-pieces and organ-shutters commissioned around 1578 for the church of San Giacomo on the glass-makers' island of Murano. Three of them were acquired for Burghley House in 1691 and still hang there, one is in the Barber Institute at the University of Birmingham and the other has been lost.

This one – *The Resurrection* – was bought in Venice by Sir James Wright in 1761 and brought to England; then, for more than a century and a half, it hung in Lowther Castle, the Earl of Lonsdale's seat. Sold in 1947 and acquired by the dealers, Colnaghi, it was bought for the Westminster Hospital in 1950 for what now seems an amazingly modest price of £9,000, of which £2,000 was raised by public subscription. It was then loaned for special exhibitions at the Royal Academy, in Birmingham, in Manchester and at the National Gallery in Athens. When the Westminster closed in 1993, it was brought to Chelsea.

In 1996, the painting was sent for restoration to the studio of Carol Willoughby and Paul Ackroyd, who were advised by the restorer Herbert Lank and the Veronese scholar, Dr Richard Cocke of the University of East Anglia. Restoration has revealed the painting in its original glory and the tradition of rich colour in the tradition of Bellini and Titian. The sight of it lifts the spirits and may help to heal the body.

1997

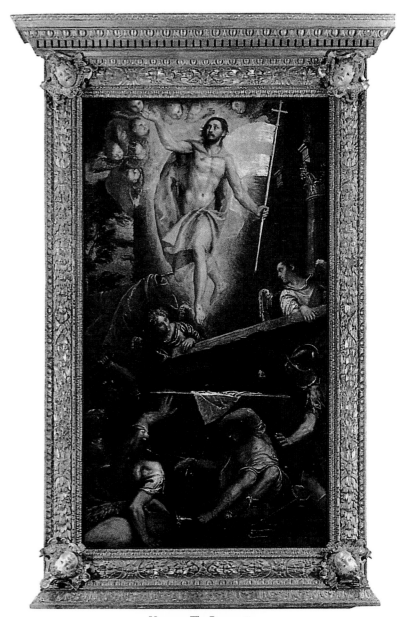

Veronese: The Resurrection

Danvers House

——

David Le Lay

Chelsea has over the centuries seen many fine and accomplished buildings, yet it cannot be said that any of them have been of seminal importance; except that is for Danvers House. For a relatively brief period, from 1623 until about 1700, there existed a house and garden that had an enormous influence upon the future of both architecture and garden design in this country. Samuel Pepys visited the house, declaring it 'the prettiest contrived house that I ever saw in my life' and John Aubrey was so impressed that he wrote a detailed description of house and garden and made sketches of the garden.

Fortunately, there is plenty of documentary evidence as to the appearance of the garden but less so in respect of the house. An attempt at a 'reconstruction' of the house and garden, using Kip's famous 1699 engraving of Beaufort House as a base, appears with this article.

Throughout the sixteenth and seventeenth centuries members of the aristocracy, and indeed the King himself, built substantial mansions on the banks of the Thames, both upstream and downstream of Chelsea village and its old church. Sir Thomas More built himself such a house in 1521, upstream of Chelsea village, with very extensive gardens and grounds. During the seventeenth century, as Chelsea became ever more popular as a place for the nobility to reside, parts of the grounds of the house were sold off. One such site was purchased by Sir John Danvers in 1622 from the then owner of Thomas More's house, the 3rd Earl of Lincoln.

Sir John Danvers Kt. (1588-1655) was the third and youngest son of Sir John Danvers Bt. By all accounts he was an exceedingly handsome and attractive young man. He was highly intelligent and travelled widely in France and Italy where he became well-versed in all the arts. He was knighted by James I and under Charles I became a high ranking courtier, being a 'gentleman of the privy chamber'. The impression is gained however that he was all too aware of his fine attributes, probably rather arrogant and not above using people for his own ends.

He married three times; firstly, when he was only 20, Magdalen Herbert, a widow more than twice his age and mother of ten children, including George Herbert, the poet and hymn writer. When she died, in 1627, he married Elizabeth Dauntsey who brought him a country estate, Lavington in Wiltshire, where he laid out gardens even more elaborate than those in Chelsea. She bore him two daughters but died in 1636 aged only 32. His third marriage, in 1649, was to another widow, Grace Hewes by whom he had a further son.

As a younger son, Sir John could not expect a substantial inheritance and his extravagant tastes led to debt and endless struggles with creditors, notwithstanding the fortune owned by his second wife. He was a Member of Parliament for most of his adult life. When civil war broke out he supported the parliamentary cause and he was a member of the commission that tried Charles I in 1649, and a signatory to his death-warrant.

Sir John Danvers' house at Chelsea was one of the earliest examples of Italian renaissance design to be carried out in England. The plan of the house, with its symmetry and centralised unity closely resembles Palladio's villa plans that were to become so popular in England a century later. There is no record as to who the designer was, though the name of lnigo Jones has often been put forward as a possible contender. Although it is quite possible that Jones was consulted, it is most likely that the design was largely the work of Sir John Danvers himself.

The most notable feature of the house itself was the main hall that was raised well above the surrounding ground level and extended the full depth of the building, allowing for both a view of the river and the distant Surrey hills to the south and of the garden to the north. This hall was approached from a broad flight of stairs leading up from the entrance hall below. In order not to interrupt the vista, and in the interests of symmetry, access to the main drawing room directly above was by means of two long flights of stairs, one on either side – thus the arrangement of stairs is one of the first instances of what is known as an 'imperial staircase' to be found in England.

Although not a particularly large house, it included a chapel and a music room with a fine organ; it was a house intended for entertainment and for show. The building also incorporated four large balustraded viewing platforms, one in each corner as well as another on top of the main central block; all of these once again affording extensive views of the garden, the river and the surrounding countryside.

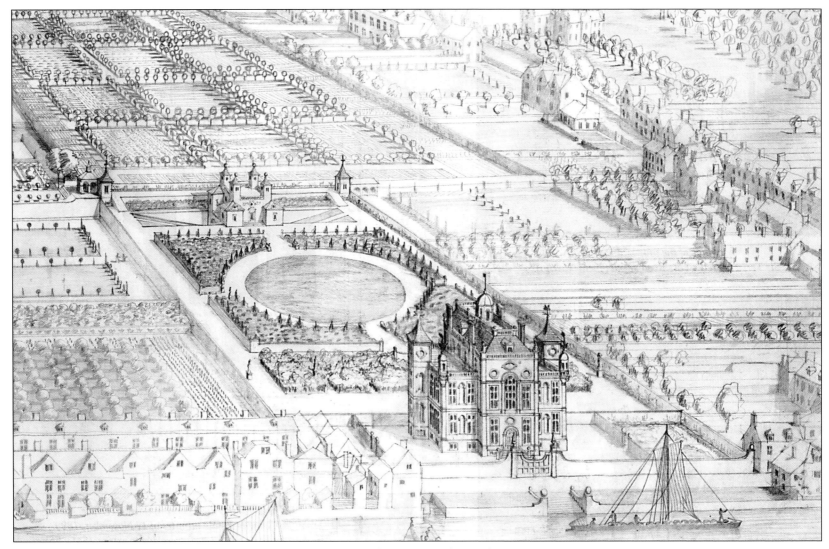

Reconstruction of Danvers House by David Le Lay

The garden, with its enclosing walls and multi levels is reminiscent of many a villa outside Rome or Florence. Probably most remarkable of all is the way in which the house and garden were conceived as a single design, a notion then unknown in England. In this, and in other ways, Danvers House is most closely related to the Villa Giulia, Rome, designed by Vignola in 1550.

The garden was divided into three distinct parts. The main steps from the house, divided into two flights upon entering the garden, each being confronted by an evocation of a wilderness comprising two rectangular areas planted with dense shrubs and fruit trees. Within each area, narrow paths lead to a statue in the middle, the gardener on one side and his wife on the other. There was a wall across the central path between these areas, so as to conceal the remainder of the garden behind.

Having left this wilderness one emerged upon the main paths along the east and west sides, which were terminated by pavilions at the north end and statues at the south end, near to the wilderness. These statues, each depicted two figures in conflict, one of Cain and Abel, the other Hercules and Antaeus. John Aubrey tells us that all the many statues throughout the garden were carved in stone by Nicholas Stone, the leading sculptor of the day, and they were coloured to make them as realistic as possible.

The central area was dominated by a perfect oval bowling green, enclosed within a rectangular wall with pairs of statues at the entrances depicting shepherds and shepherdesses. The quadrant areas were densely planted with shrubs and edged with closely-spaced formal clipped evergreens. In each corner of the enclosing wall there were small pavilions with flat roofs.

The part of the garden furthest from the house was dominated by a raised terrace, with the pavilions referred to earlier at each end. In front of the terrace was a banqueting room with corner staircase towers giving access to a flat roof over. Below this banqueting room was a grotto. The raised terrace and sunken grotto were approached by means of gentle ramps. From both the terrace and the roof of the banqueting room one could look back over the garden towards the house.

It can be seen that the garden represented, in a stylised way, a progression from a wilderness with shades of the garden of Eden, to an Elysian arcady with its perfect lawn and happy shepherds, and ending with perhaps 'multi-level' present day reality – the banqueting room hovering between the hell of the grotto and the elevated heavenly towers above. Whatever one's particular interpretation, the garden was certainly designed to produce particular sensations in a specific sequence and it consciously embodied an allegorical and psychological approach to garden design which was unique in its day.

The creation of various levels at the north end of the garden, including the sunken grotto, with a complex system of circulation between each level is similar to that at the Villa Giulia in Rome. Although the land on which Sir John Danvers created his garden was generally flat, he was helped, or possibly inspired, by the raised terrace that already existed. This had been formed a century earlier under the direction of Sir Thomas More who soon after occupying his new house had decided to erect a new building with a private study, away from the house, and to which he could escape from his large family, for peace and quiet. The terrace was constructed to provide an elevated walk to the new building which could well have been on the site of Sir John Danvers' banqueting room, or Sir John might even have adapted and altered More's 'new building' to serve this new purpose.

Sir John Danvers died in 1655, the house being inherited by one of his sons-in-law, Lord Wharton, and it was eventually sold to William Sloane, of the Sloane Stanley Estate. The house was pulled down to make way for Danvers Street, the alignment of which coincides with the central axis of the house. It is not certain exactly when this happened, but it was probably in the period 1700-10. The garden was not built over until much later, when it was combined with other land to allow for the construction of Paultons Square. The 1710 houses built on the west side of Danvers Street were not demolished until 1906, to make way for the re-erection of Crosby Hall.

It is interesting to observe that Crosby Hall, occupying as it does part of the site of Danvers House, is now a new Chelsea riverside mansion that reflects, like its predecessor, the ideas of its owner.

2002

Selected Bibliography and sources

Survey of London, Vol. IV Chelsea – Part II, published for the L.C.C. by Country Life, 1913; *Garden and Grove, The Italian Renaissance Garden in the English Imagination 1600-1750,* John Dixon Hunt, J.M. Dent & Sons Ltd, 1986; *The Renaissance Garden in England*, Roy Strong, Thames and Hudson, 1979; *Classicism without Jones*, John Harris, Country Life, October 4th 1990; *On Danvers House, Chelsea*, John Aubrey, Bodleian Library, Oxford, Aubrey MS 2 f 53 59., (Transcript in Chelsea Library, ref 1674 – 76); A Map of Chelsea in about 1706 showing water supplies to Beaufort House and the Manor House, Chelsea Library; Floor plans and sketch of front elevation of Danvers House, John Thorpe, Soane Museum.

CHELSEA CHINA

'…that fine and distingush'd Manufactory'

Sally Kevill Davies

Because England enjoyed none of the advantages of royal patronage, from which the great eighteenth-century porcelain factories of Germany and France so palpably benefited, all the English factories were set up as commercial enterprises which were forced to pay their way from the start. Indeed, the history of these early factories is punctuated with the stories of fortunes, lives and reputations ruined by the obsessive quest for the secret of 'true' or hard-paste porcelain, as made in China, Japan and Germany. Chelsea is the first English factory recorded as having made porcelain, but it was an 'artificial' or 'soft-paste' porcelain similar to that made in France at Vincennes and later Sèvres, where a body more akin to glass than porcelain was used. Confirmation that success had been achieved was publicised in the *Daily Advertiser*, 5 March, 1745. 'We hear that China made at Chelsea is arriv'd to such Perfection, as to equal if not surpass the finest old Japan, allow'd so by the most approv'd Judges here; and that the same is in so high Esteem of the Nobility and the Demand so great, that a sufficient Quantity can hardly be made to answer the Call for it'.

The factory was set up in a number of converted dwelling-houses in the riverside village of Chelsea, under the artistic *aegis* of Nicholas Sprimont, a young Huguenot silversmith from Liège. Chelsea was a pleasant spot noted, in the middle of the eighteenth century, for its good air and market gardens, and the country home of Sir Hans Sloane, the celebrated physician, scientist and collector. The proximity of Ranelagh Gardens, and Vauxhall a short wherry ride away on the opposite bank, attracted the *beau-monde*, while Don Saltero's Coffee House was a convivial meeting place where literary and artistic matters could be discussed by the likes of Tobias Smollett and Louis-François Roubiliac.

Chelsea's Ranelagh was considered the most exclusive of London's eighteenth century pleasure gardens. The *beau-monde* gathered there during the summer months for ballooning, fireworks and 'spectacles', for concerts, gaming, dancing and dining, but, most importantly, to see and to be seen. As Horace Walpole succinctly remarked in 1742, the year in which the Rotunda was opened, 'Nobody goes anywhere else, everybody goes there'.

Ranelagh was the scene of numerous *masques* and entertainments, where a black *domino* pulled across the face, obliterated the identity of revellers and performers alike, adding to the air of delicious mystery. The night of 24 May 1759 saw one such masque, held to celebrate the birthday of Frederick, Prince of Wales. Chelsea figures were traditionally held to portray characters from that masque, though none corresponds exactly with the figures in the prints made to commemorate the occasion, by Bowles after Maurer.

The early Chelsea wares, made between 1745 and 1749, at a time when Sprimont was still continuing with his work as a silversmith, were mainly left in the white or sparsely decorated in enamels, but all show an individualistic treatment of the French Rococo style, used by Sprimont and other contemporary Huguenot silversmiths. They bear the triangle mark incised, the triangle being the alchemist's sign for Fire. During this period Sprimont is known to have received financial assistance from Sir Everard Fawkener, the brother of the Governor of the Bank of England, and Secretary to the Duke of Cumberland.

For about a year, between 1749 and 1750, Sprimont closed down his rapidly expanding business, during which time he moved to larger, purpose-built premises facing onto Lawrence Street. When he re-opened for business he proclaimed that his wares were 'in a Taste entirely new' and for the next decade the Chelsea factory prospered. At first, the mark used was an anchor in relief on a small pad of clay. It has been suggested that this may be a rebus of Sprimont's name, the 'Spri', or 'Spre' as it is sometimes misspelt represented by the anchor of Hope (the Latin for 'I Hope' is 'Spero'), and the 'mont' represented by the small 'mount', or pad of clay on which the anchor is set. In 1752, the mark changed to a less cumbersome anchor painted in red enamel.

With the move to Lawrence Street, the formula of the paste and glaze was modified to produce a clear white, slightly opaque, surface on which to paint. Nicholas Sprimont employed a young Irishman, Jefferyes Hamett O'Neale, to paint fable scenes, as well as classical figures among Italianate ruins, Meissen-style harbour scenes and 'landskips' in the soft palette of Vincennes. In addition to O'Neale, other Chelsea artists included William Duvivier and Jean Lefèbre. In the 1750s about 100 workers were employed at

The Masqueraders

Chelsea including a 'nursery of 30 lads taken from the parishes and charity schools and bred to designing and painting'. Favourite subjects of the raised and red anchor period include Japanese-inspired subjects in the manner of the Kakiemon family of Arita, flowered in the Meissen and Vincennes style, and the outrageously flamboyant 'Hans Sloane' plants, inspired by the botanical engravings of specimens in the Chelsea Physic Garden by G. D. Ehret.

In June, 1751, Sir Everard Fawkener, a patron of the factory, wrote to his friend, Sir Charles Hanbury Williams, British Envoy in Dresden, asking him to purchase and send to London Meissen porcelain to the value of 'over fifty or three score pounds' worth in order to furnish the Undertakers (of the Chelsea factory) with good designs'. Instead, as a less costly alternative, Sir Charles magnanimously offered the Chelsea workmen access to the two Meissen services presented to him by Augustus III in 1748, which were being stored, pending his return to England, at Holland House.

It is probable that the service now in the Collection of the Duke of Northumberland at Alnwick Castle was one of Sir Charles's Meissen services, pieces of which were copied at Chelsea.

The Rococo style originated in France during the early 18th century, and found a ready market in mid-eighteenth century England. Nervous, playful and full of asymmetrical curves and scrolls which suggested natural elements such as flames, rocks, shells and water, the style was particularly successful when applied to the decorative arts, furniture, silver and, above all, porcelain. The burgeoning middle-classes, anxious to display their new-found wealth, indulged in a bout of rampant consumerism, and English craftsmen and designers, eager to dispel the myth that, in the arts, France was in the ascendant, strove to supply the demand for luxury goods.

Like Nicholas Sprimont, many of the artists and craftsmen were Huguenots who, forced to flee after the Revocation of the Edict of Nantes, brought to England a French sophistication and dedication to high standards of workmanship.

At Chelsea during the gold anchor period, the influence of Sèvres, with its sumptuous colour grounds and lavish gilding, was particularly strong, since production at Meissen had all but ceased during the Seven Years' War (1757-63). The Rococo *brio* engendered and enjoyed by 'the whipped cream of Europe' as Voltaire described his country, was *de rigueur* where taste and money talked.

For figure models, Sprimont employed Joseph Willems, who was born in Brussels in 1715, and worked at Tournai until his arrival in Chelsea in c.1749. Whether they are copies of sophisticated Meissen pieces, or models adapted from engravings and larger pieces of sculpture, his figures show men and women of sturdy build, with the placid, amiable features of the Low Countries. Willems was probably responsible for all the modelling at Chelsea until his return to Tournai in 1766.

Known as 'toys', small, costly and impeccably fashioned objects were popular with the members of London's *beau* and *demi-monde* throughout the latter half of the 1750s and the 1760s. Often mounted in gold, they were just the sort of fashionable luxuries which would have appealed to the customers whom Nicholas

Sprimont was striving to attract, 'the Quality' and 'the Nobility'. Known in Germany as *Galanteriewaren*, in France as *objets de vertu* and at Chelsea as 'toys', they represented the kind of exquisite trifles which a gentleman would have presented to his affianced, his wife or his mistress. *Bonbonnières*, for *cachous* flavoured with violets to sweeten the breath, thimble-cases and *étuis*, or 'twees' as they were described in the catalogues and advertisements, to hold a lady's needles, scent bottles to contain fragrances to perfume the wearer when personal hygiene was inclined to be basic, and seals to dangle from a *châtelaine*, to ensure the privacy of a *billet doux*. Many bore witty French mottoes (often charmingly misspelt), to add to the frisson of a double-entendre, or just a certain Gallic '*je ne sais quoi*'.

1999

DOWN THE GARDEN PATHS...

Kenwyn Pearson,
former Head Gardener to the Cadogan Estate

In the early 1990s, we are all too well aware of the effects of traffic and the increasing demand on our space. But in Chelsea we are lucky to have a good proportion of open space and gardens and trees which help to filter noise and reduce pollution. Also in Chelsea many private properties have well-established gardens in which the owners take pride. So I would like to muse for a while on how Chelsea has evolved horticulturally.

The manor of Chelsea, acquired by King Henry VIII in the 1530s, had a great garden, which, as seen on a map by James Hamilton of 1664, was planted with bays, cherries, nut trees, damsons, peaches, 200 damask roses, whitethorn and privet hedges. It also employed 29 gardeners and six women weeders. Equal opportunities did not form part of 16th century legislation.

The Royal Hospital had not been built, and the King's Road was completed for Charles II to drive from Whitehall to the Old Fulham Ferry, mentioned in Domesday Book, en route for Putney and his palace at Hampton Court, where the gardens were being restyled in the fashionable French style. All the land now bounded by Old Church Street, Beaufort Street, the Fulham Road and the Thames was the great garden of Sir Thomas More and goes back into history before the Physic Garden came into existence. More's garden was visited by Erasmus and Holbein and had a wide range of shrubs. More grew rosemary in abundance. In the north-east corner stood the great elm known as the Queen's Elm, beneath which Queen Elizabeth I supposedly sheltered from a rainstorm while walking with Lord Burleigh. By 1625 More's garden had been incorporated in Chelsea Park and by 1876 it was built over by the Elm Park Estate.

The Chelsea Physic Garden came into being in 1673 with the lease of 3 and a half acres from Lord Cheyne to form the garden of the Apothecaries. The famous cedars of Lebanon were planted in about 1683 and the high wall surrounding it was built to prevent theft of specimens. This wall enabled an even greater range of plants to be grown and the large stove-greenhouse was built in the garden in 1681.

The arrival of Hans Sloane on the scene in 1684 was to significantly change horticulture in Chelsea, particularly in the Physic Garden and in the progressive development of the Cadogan Estate and, indeed, the whole world of horticulture.

The Manor of Chelsea survived in various forms and with additions and changes until it was sold to Charles Cheyne in 1667. In 1698 it passed to his son, and he sold the entire estate and Manor to Sir Hans Sloane in 1712. This signalled the end of the old Chelsea and the beginning of a new era, some of which survives to the present day. It was through the marriage of one of Sloane's daughters, Elizabeth, to the second Lord Cadogan that the Cadogans came into possession of a large part of Chelsea.

Horticulturally the next major period of change came through Henry Holland, the architect. In the 1770s he was working as an assistant to "Capability" Brown, the famous landscaper, and made an approach to Lord Cadogan with plans for a new development. Holland then leased about 100 acres of what was to become Hans Town in the area we now know as Sloane Street, Sloane Square, Hans Place, Cadogan Square and Cadogan Place. In his proposed development he reserved himself 21 acres on the west side of the land, near what we now know as Pavilion Road, and here he erected an elegant house and planted gardens. It was supposedly from this design that, in 1787, he built the first Brighton Pavilion designed as a classical villa.

In the 1770s, market gardens were gaining in importance and Jacques Poupart developed one on what is now the Chelsea Football Ground at Stamford Bridge. Then there was the Royal Exotic Nursery near to what is now South Kensington underground station, which, trading under the name of Wills and Segar, sold palms, pot plants and floral arrangements to the large houses of London, including Buckingham Palace. Knight and Perry later ran the nursery until 1853 when Veitch took it over.

Holland died in 1806 and the Pavilion was sold to a Peter Denys. The population of Chelsea continued to rise as London expanded and took up more of the surrounding villages. This development had made Holland realise the potential of the area, but it was also this that eventually destroyed most of the green spaces. About 14 acres of land to the west of the Pavilion was leased in the mid-19th century as market gardens and nurseries but the development of Cadogan Square and Lennox Gardens was soon to change this. The market gardens sold their produce to residents in Hans Town and people who lived nearer the river in the ever-growing Cadogan Estate. Slowly the market gardens were pushed out of the area and the land was taken over for recreation, or ornamental gardens. These became the London squares and private gardens we know today.

One of the largest private gardens in Chelsea surviving to this day is on Sloane Street and known as Cadogan Place Garden. As a private garden, this was fenced towards the end of the 18th. century, when a London Botanic Garden was formed by a man named Salisbury. This covered six acres, and included a library, hot house, greenhouse and conservatory. In 1807, the plants were labelled and the full details of the garden were revealed in the August edition of *The Gentleman's Magazine* in 1810. Horticultural students attended lectures there and from May to September concerts were held in the gardens; subscribers to the garden living within one mile paid 11 guineas per year for membership. In 1991, the garden measured 7.5 acres, cost over £100, 000 a year to maintain and was run by 21 gardeners. The range of plantings and species has changed substantially not least because of the problems of Dutch Elm disease and the storm of 1987. But most of the existing framework of the garden, the lawns, paths and shrubberies has not changed for over 100 years.

Kenwyn Pearson in a Chelsea garden

Paultons Square was built in the 1830s on a market garden and named after Paultons in Hampshire, the country seat of George Stanley, Sir Hans Sloane's son-in-law, and, of course, survives as a garden. Markham Square which was laid out in 1836 was built on a field, which was part of what was known as Box Farm. Chelsea Square was renamed in the 1920s, being previously Trafalgar Square, long before the famous one in Westminster and has an interesting square garden. The famous Chelsea Rectory garden, dating back to 1566, contains mulberries said to have been planted in the reign of Queen Elizabeth I; there are other mulberries in Chelsea planted during the reign of Charles II.

Lennox Gardens was built on Prince's Cricket Ground after its lease had expired in 1885. Oakley Street and Oakley Gardens have strong gardening links and Oakley Square, renamed Carlyle Square in 1872 in honour of Thomas Carlyle, was built on a market garden. In 1851, Dr. J. S. Phené, who built Carlton Terrace and Phene Street, planted many of the trees which survive in that area today. Part of the wide boulevard of Royal Avenue, built to connect the Chelsea Hospital with Kensington Palace, but never completed beyond the Kings Road, survives today. Chelsea also has squares, churchyards and gardens maintained by residents' associations and individuals for the benefit of the community.

And so to the future. It is most important that the cities of the world keep and maintain their open spaces, trees and landscapes and we should follow the lead of many countries, particularly on the Continent, and encourage patios, pots, containers and window-box gardening. Elm Disease and the storm of 1987 presented a wonderful challenge to us all for change and development. The Clean Air Acts have done much to reduce the effects of pollution, and modern hybridizers, plant breeders and plant collectors have vastly increased our awareness of horticulture and the range of plants available.

1991

CREMORNE GARDENS

Edward Croft-Murray, C.B.E.

The London Pleasure Gardens were essentially a creation of the eighteenth century. But their tradition lingered well into Victorian times: Vauxhall, doyen of them all, did not finally close till 1859; and Cremorne, subject of the present paper, was virtually a Victorian institution, being opened as a Pleasure Garden in 1843 and coming to an end in 1877.

Like several other Pleasure Gardens, including Ranelagh – its Georgian counterpart in Chelsea – and of course Vauxhall, Cremorne started life as a Thames-side country house. The property occupied a site between the west end of the King's Road and the River: more precisely it was bounded on the east by what was then known as Cremorne Lane, now Dartrey Road; on the south by the present Lots Road; and on the west by the present Uverdale Road. The World's End tavern stood - and still stands - at what was its north-east angle on the King's Road; and its entrance, through a handsome pair of wrought-iron gates (shown in an etching by Walter Greaves of 1871) was opposite the area known as Ten Acre Field now occupied by the attractive mid-Victorian layout which includes Hobury Street, Limerston Street, Stanley Villas and Lamont Road.

Cremorne House itself – originally known as Chelsea Farm-stood at the River end of the property. It was built by Theophilus Hastings, 9th Earl of Huntingdon (1696–1746), husband of the foundress of the famous Calvinistic 'connection'. It seems to have been by the early nineteenth century, a pleasant – if rather undistinguished – late-Georgian building; but the grounds were finally landscaped into sweeping lawns backed by richly planted trees. The property subsequently passed to a succession of aristocratic owners: one of the Viscounts Powerscourt; a Countess Dowager of Exeter; Sir Richard Littleton; the 3rd Duke of Bridgewater; and Thomas Dawson, 1st Viscount Cremorne (1725–1813) – his title derived from one of the Baronies of Co. Monaghan – who (according to Wheatley and Cunningham) 'spent a large sum on the house, placed in it a fine collection of pictures, and greatly improved the

Whistler at Cremorne Gardens by Walter Greaves

grounds'. It was after him, of course, that the property was in future to be called. In 1770, he had married, as his second wife, an American lady, Philadelphia Hannah, daughter of Thomas Freame of Philadelphia and granddaughter of William Penn, founder of that city. She died in 1826, leaving the property to her cousin, Grenville Penn, its last private owner. It was sold by him in 1830.

Its purchaser was a colourful figure who in spirit belongs more, perhaps, to the eighteenth century than to the nineteenth: his full style, the 'Baron' Charles Random de Berenger, indeed, has a Smollett-like ring about it. Through him Cremorne was to take on a new existence. The Baron's speciality was firearms for which he is said to have taken out innumerable patents – an example of his art, a double-barrelled gun, specially made to his design 'for preventing accidents', is still preserved in the Chelsea Public Library. Cremorne was opened by him in 1831 as a Stadium or Sports Club where gentlemen, for a membership fee of 2-3 guineas, could shoot, box or fence under his tuition. A lithograph by W. Day and Charles, *The Stadium at Chelsea*, published in the year of its opening, shows a company of gentlemen in quasi-military uniform, with their rifles, grouped before an elegant striped pavilion, the extensive lawns and clumps of trees of Cremorne stretching away around them. The Baron also anticipated, by a century, the amenities of certain

London Clubs of today by providing a 'Ladies' Annexe' – rather more exclusive than its twentieth century counterpart – where gentlemen could not enter except 'by consent of the Ladies occupying such'. By 1834 the Stadium's activities had been extended to include pole-jumping and golf, these sports being symbolized on a shield designed for it by George Cruickshank.

Random de Berenger was succeeded at Cremorne, in c. 1843-5 by another 'Baron' of even more dubious nobility, Renton Nicholson, writer on sport and proprietor of the Garrick's Head in Bow Street, where he had achieved the title of 'Lord Chief Baron Nicholson' by staging a series of mock trials which became very popular as entertainment. He, in his turn, was followed by the well-known pantomime clown Tom Matthews who managed the Gardens for a year in 1846.

Cremorne's golden age as a place of entertainment can be said to have started with Matthew's successor, James Ellis, under whom the grounds were first brought in line with the traditional layout of a London Pleasure Garden. They were further developed in this direction by Thomas Bartlett Simpson, former head-waiter at the Albion Tavern opposite Drury Lane Theatre, who took over from Ellis in 1849 or '50, after the latter's bankruptcy. T. B. Simpson (not to be confused with the famous Regency Master of Ceremonies at Vauxhall, C. H. Simpson) reigned at Cremorne till 1861, and during his time there, in 1850, increased the size of the property by taking in part of the grounds of the neighbouring Ashburnham House.

A vivid contrast is provided by the plan of Cremorne in F. P. Thompson's *Map of Chelsea* of 1836, in which its house, its lawns and plantations alone are indicated, and that in the *Ordnance Survey* of 1865 (published in 1867) where the area is crowded with all the impedimenta which would have been familiar to the *habitués* of Vauxhall: 'orchestra', supper-boxes, theatres, firework-gallery and the rest. But much of its original qualities as a landscape-garden would also have been preserved; and even outside its boundaries at this time there were still extensive market-gardens. The journalist George Augustus Sala recalled the Cremorne of Simpson's day as 'a real pleasaunce surrounded by magnificent trees, with well-kept lawns and lovely flowers, and melodious singing birds', and that 'nothing was pleasanter in the summer-time than to saunter in at midday or the early afternoon (for the Gardens were not properly open till three or five), and find Mr. Simpson's daughters there with their workbaskets – to say nothing of the pretty barmaids employed by the kindly and generous gentleman, who were busy in their cotton frocks, arranging the bars'.

Walter Greaves's delightful Cremorne etchings of 1870-71 depict some of the buildings erected by Ellis and Simpson, all of which are of an appropriately Brighton Pavilionish exoticism. Most prominent was the 'Orchestra', a huge bandstand (already installed by Ellis in his short reign of 1846-9) which was obviously modelled on the famous Moorish-Gothic structure (dating from 1758) at Vauxhall, but seemingly in more 'correct' Chinese taste-the 'Pagoda' of the Ordnance Survey. The Firework-Gallery, on the other hand, evidently veered more towards *turquerie*, and was flanked by minarets. There were theatres, a circus, a 'Gipsy's Tent', a Maze, and – highly up-to-date – an 'American bowling-saloon' where 'American drinks' were served, this last-mentioned being installed in 1848-9.

Entrance was a shilling a head; and a season ticket cost 1-2 guineas. Though attempts were made to attract the same kind of aristocratic patronage which had been accorded to the Georgian gardens in their heyday, Cremorne never seems to have caught on in this respect. The clientele was essentially the London "cit" and his family (efforts were made to attract the young Victorian 'master' and 'miss' besides their 'papa' and 'mama'), as well as the *midinettes* and their boy-friends.

Something of the decorum and etiquette of the older Gardens persisted, at least at the beginning, and a Master of Ceremonies was in attendance. A half-crown cold supper was provided, and a favourite beverage was the Cremorne sherry which was guaranteed to be 'free from acidity, and highly recommended to invalids'. Transport was also available: 'Steamers, and Omnibusses, every ten minutes', are announced on an early bill; and Cremorne had its own pier where those who arrived by water could disembark, while those who came by land entered by the grand gates on the King's Road 'where a big star illuminated the pay-box'. Some of the actual entertainments devised by Ellis and Simpson and their successors will be noted separately below.

Simpson retired in 1861; but ownership of the Gardens was retained by him, and by his family after his death in 1872. In 1861 the management was taken over by Edward Tyrrell Smith. He is said to have been the son of a naval commander, Admiral E. T. Smith; but, despite this distinguished parentage, he started his working life in a comparatively humble capacity, first as a Bow Street Runner and then as an Inspector in the newly formed Metropolitan Police Force. In 1850, after spells as a Sheriff's Officer and an auctioneer, he became landlord of a tavern in Red Lion Street, Holborn, 'attracting custom by dressing his barmaids in bloomer costume'. He then turned his attention to theatre-management, including that of Drury Lane and Her Majesty's, and in 1852-3 built the Alhambra in Leicester Square. His régime at Cremorne lasted till 1869. One of its minor, but engaging features, noted by Wroth, would have been the issue of 'charming little folding programmes... printed in colours, and presenting on every page a view of Cremorne'. These must have looked rather like the pictorial Valentines of the period, portions being 'ingeniously cut out, so that on the front page there was a view up the long walk, flanked by trees and lamp-bearing goddesses, right up to the great fountain'.

Cremorne's last *impresario* was John Baum. For a while the Gardens seem to have flourished under his care, and numerous bills and programmes testify to the variety of entertainment provided by him for his customers. He, too, issued pictorial programmes; not as elaborate as those provided by Smith, but nevertheless very prettily embellished with pen-lithographic title-pages and borders to the text illustrating scenes from the ballet and other attractions. But Cremorne – like Vauxhall in its latter days – began to build up a reputation for rowdiness and other misdemeanours, which Baum found difficult to control. Indeed, its reputation lived on after its demise, in Paul Marriott's melodrama of *New Babylon*, staged at the Duke's Theatre, Holborn, in 1879, in which the theme of Act I, 'The Road to Ruin', was symbolized by scenes at "Tattersalls" and "Cremorne". Already in 1857 the Chelsea Vestry had tried unsuccessfully to prevent the renewal of the Cremorne licence; and henceforth this was to be a perennial practice on the part of that body. By the 1870's its members were supported in their efforts by a sturdy pillar of the Church, Canon Cromwell, Principal of the neighbouring St. Mark's Training College, who was pilloried for his pains by a cartoon, in *The Day's Doings* for November 11th, 1871, representing him, in cap and gown, 'progging' (to use an Oxbridge colloquialism) two of the Cremorne tarts. In 1876 came a riposte from the side of the Vestry: a verse-pamphlet, *The Trial of John Fox, or Fox John, or the Horrors of Cremorne*, directed at Baum. The author was another churchman, Alfred Brandon, minister of Chelsea Baptist Church. Baum won the ensuing libel-action, but was only awarded a farthing damages. The licence was applied for, but Baum by this time was ill and badly in debt and decided to withdraw it. And so Cremorne came to an end: its fate will be told in the Epilogue below.

Already during the later years of Baron Random de Berenger's

essentially athletic and sporting regime Cremorne had begun to take on some of the character for which it was to be famed in High Victorian times: in 1836, there were firework displays by Messrs. Duffell and Darby; in 1838-40, various *fêtes champêtres* were held; there were balloon-ascents and Parachute-drops by Mrs. Graham and John Hampton; and in 1839, 'Charles Random was granted a license for music and dancing.'

Programmes also survive from the period of Tom Matthews and his successor James Ellis in the 1840's to show that they provided their clientele with Ballet, Pantomime, Farce and Vaudeville, *al fresco* dancing and various musical performances.

Aeronautic displays were – as they had been in the Georgian Gardens – among the more spectacular events in Cremorne life. In the mid-1840's, there were ascents by the veteran balloonist, Charles Green, one being in company with 'a lady and a leopard', and another with Lord George Beresford and the then manager, Tom Matthews, who preluded the take-off with a performance of his famous ditty *Hot Codlings*. On August 23rd, 1845, Green made a 'Night Ascent', with some kind of firework dangling from below the basket; and on June 29th, 1846, announced that he would take 'A Large Party' up in 'the Great Nassau', the car being an elegant boat-shaped construction with an eagle-headed finial at either end.

There followed in the 1850's a group of intrepid French aeronauts: Bouthellier who executed a trapeze act attached to the car of a balloon; Madame Poitevin who on one occasion ascended *en amazonne*, mounted 'on her favourite steed Zampa', and on another, 'in the character of Europa', astride a heifer – she and Simpson, the manager, were subsequently fined, on September 9th, 1852, for 'cruelty to animals'; and Henri Latour, another veteran, who in his fiftieth year tried his luck, on a parachute shaped 'like a horse' which was attached to W. H. Adams's balloon, but came to grief and was killed.

Another Frenchman, M. Delamarne, appeared in 1865 with an early form of dirigible, 'The Aereal Vessel or Sailing Baloon [*sic*]! "L'Esperance" ' which (according to the woodcut accompanying the announcement) was evidently propelled by two paddle-wheels rotating on either side of the cylindrical air-bag and worked by hand from the car below. Another kind of early aerial transport presumably anticipated the overhead railway. Billed in 1848 as 'The Aerial Steam Carriage', it ran 'in a commodious covered way, extending upward of 400 feet in length'. 'The Model Carriages', it was claimed, would be 'worked entirely by Steam, without the aid of

Gas', and would 'illustrate the preliminary steps of this scientific and wondrous movement of the age'.

In 1869, a French 'captive balloon' was installed at Cremorne, in which members of the public were allowed to ascend in a car capable of holding thirty passengers and of rising to a height of 2,000 feet. The charge was 10/- a head; but an exception was made in the case of 'a female inmate of Fulham Workhouse'. She was appropriately given a free trip, for with splendid courage she had elected to celebrate her hundredth birthday by the ascent.

The Cremorne Gates

But by far the most spectacular of the Cremorne aeronauts would have been the Belgian 'flying man' Vincent De Groof. According to Wroth, he had already made 'some ascents with doubtful success in his native land' before his arrival in England in 1874. He appeared at Cremorne on the evening of June 29th of that year. His machine was made of 'cane and waterproof silk... in imitation of the bat's wing and peacock's tail'. The span of the wings was 37 feet and the tail 18 feet long. In the middle was a platform on which its inventor stood and worked the wings and tail by means of three levers. Initial ascent was attained by attachment to a balloon, in this instance named the 'Czar'. The 'flying man' had intended to land in the Gardens, but the 'Czar' carried him away to Brandon in Suffolk where he made a 'perilous but successful descent'. The Cremorne connoisseurs of aeronautic displays demanded another attempt, and this was announced for July 9th by a large and effective poster exhibiting a pen-lithograph of De Groof confidently and dramatically sailing over London on his own. Alas, nothing like this happened. After the initial take-off, the 'Czar' and De Groof hovered for about half-an-hour over the Gardens and then were blown perilously near the tower of St. Luke's Church where it was decided to cut De Groof adrift. The luckless 'flying man' and his contrivance fell 'with a heavy thud near the curbstone in Robert [Sydney] St.' He was rushed to the Chelsea Infirmary where he died from his injuries. Meanwhile the 'Czar' was again carried away eastwards, this time towards Springfield in Essex where it came down on the Great Eastern line and narrowly missed a passing train. The disaster was celebrated in a typical Cockney ballad of the time, 'Sung and sold by two Men in Slone [sic] Square Monday Evening July 13th, 1874', and beginning 'you feeling hearts list to my story...', and The *Illustrated Police News* headed its opening sheet with three wood-engravings of *The Start from Cremorne*, *The Fall*, and *The Death*.

We may also recall at random some of the other – and, perhaps, rather less hazardous of the Cremorne entertainments. Fêtes were a regular feature. In 1846, Cremorne nostalgically paid homage to Ranelagh, its Georgian predecessor, by staging a Public Breakfast during which catches and glees by Dr. Arne, *doyen* of Pleasure Garden composers, were 'performed by the Grandest Vocal and Instrumental Concert ever introduced to public approbation'; while further antique flavour was achieved by 'Dances of the period, and in the costume of the time of Ranelagh's Zenith,' and by 'sturdy chairmen' who would be seen 'bearing the Sedan and setting down at different points of the Gardens, Ladies of Quality and Gentlemen of Distinction' – altogether a charming expression of the Second Rococo. In 1851 was held an 'Aquatic Tournament or Naval Fête', in which a fortress (representing either St. John of Acre or Gibraltar) was attacked by a squadron of fourteen steamers of the Citizen Company, the bangs being furnished by Messrs. Mortram and Duffell, the Cremorne fireworkers. The army also had its turn: a 'Grand Military Fête... in aid of the Friends of Wellington College' – doubtless one of the very few occasions when a distinguished Public School has been financed by a London Pleasure Garden; an undated wood-engraving shows impressive lines of troops drawn up on parade while rockets arch overhead through the night sky. In 1858 came one of Cremorne's attempts to catch the Quality: the 'Aristocratic Fête' billed for July 9th. The English weather – always a hazard in the Pleasure Garden industry – behaved at its very worst, and the evening was a complete flop, as attested by *The Illustrated London News* which published on the following July 24th a cut showing the company, umbrellas up under drenching rain, watching a few of their bedraggled fellows bravely processing round the Gardens in the wake of a military band. The July of 1863 behaved rather better for the 'Cremorne Tournament' which was held in emulation of the famous Eglintown Tournament of 1839. Here again the *I.L.N.* for July 18th, 1863, provides us with a visual document of the spectacle: knights vigorously jousting before a grandstand filled with ladies in mediaeval dress, but, whereas the Eglintown Lords and Ladies were genuine, the Cremorne participants mostly came from the Circus and the Stage – the Queen of Beauty was Madame Cardine, a celebrated trick rider of the day, and the pages are said to have been ladies who were 'no strangers to the choreographic stage'.

Conjuring and juggling were on the Cremorne menu in the mid-1840's: 'De Vere The Renowned Prestigitateur, Humourist and Anti-Spiritualist' who performed in his 'Bijou Theatre', (near the King's Road Entrance), and who (according to the woodcut on his bill) apparently produced from his hat – in place of the customary rabbit – a life-sized ballerina; and Mr. Silvani, 'the principal Acrobat of the Troupe now performing at Cremorne Gardens', who is seen balancing on his chin models of two men o' war, representing the *Chesapeake* and *Shannon*, each firing off broadsides at the other. Ordeals by Fire and Water also provided entertainment: in 1858 'Cristoforo Buono Core', the 'Italian Salamander', entered 'a burning furnace with apparent unconcern' – the I.L.N. for

September 18th shows that he achieved this by wearing some kind of protective cloak and a hood with eye-slits, in which he walked beneath a blazing pergola; and in 1867 appeared 'Natutor', the 'man-frog', who was exhibited in a glass-fronted tank of water where he 'stood on his head, ate a sponge-cake, or smoked a pipe'. Finally we may note in the *Penny Illustrated Paper*, for June 10th, 1865, a touching wood-engraving of Monsieur Lecomte, 'exhibiting his performing Sea-bear'; he, in the guise of a French *matelot*, looking down at his charge who, with flippers on his master's knees, gazes up affectionately at him with spaniel-like eyes.

In the Victorian Pleasure Gardens music played a less distinguished part than it had done in Georgian times. There were no illustrious composers to replace Arne and John Christian Bach – or even James Hook and Sir Henry Rowley Bishop – and to carry on the tradition of the rather special brand of music which they had supplied for the Garden – clientele of their day. And there certainly was no one, in London at the time, of the personality of Hans Christian Lumbye, the 'Danish Strauss', whose compositions lent such sparkle to the early years of his native 'Tivoli', Copenhagen's equivalent of Vauxhall (founded in 1843, and still happily in existence).

But perhaps most famous in the Cremorne bill of musical fare was its dancing 'al fresco' which was advertised to 'the Votaries of Terpsichore' in grandiloquent language smacking of the Music Hall. This took place on a huge circular platform surrounding the pagoda-like 'Orchestra', where (according to a lithograph of c.1850) 'Crinoline and Peg-top expose their symmetrical forms to the admiring public'. It is interesting to note that in c. 1843 'Minuets' were still being danced along with 'Quadrilles, Waltzes, Mazourkas, Polkas... and Fandangoes', the last-mentioned reflecting the taste for romantic Spain so characteristic of this period.

Instrumental music was supplied by a large orchestral band, which on occasions probably did duty for both the concerts and stage-productions as well as for the dancing, and was throughout Cremorne's existence under the direction of 'Signor Bosisio' (composer of much Victorian dance-music), Borini; and Messieurs E. Jules Rivière and Eugene Audibert – the last two being doubtless responsible for the introduction of French comic operas and other Gallic-flavoured entertainments. In 1866, 'Marriott's Great Orchestral Band' played for the dancing. There was also in the 1850's, the 'Cremorne Brass Band, conducted by Sidney Davies' (cosily advertised as playing 'on the Lawn'), and in the 1870's

'Seibold's Military Band'. Finally we may note in 1874 the visit of 'The Viennese Ladies' Orchestra… of 53 Instrumentalists, Directress Madame Almann Weinich', the strings, wind and percussion (according to a wood-engraving in *The Pictorial World* for June 20th), all elegantly laced-in and bebustled, but the brass in the backrow, suspiciously masculine-looking.

In 1878, following on the equivocal outcome of the libel-action between John Baum, the last Manager, and the Baptist Minister, Alfred Brandon, Cremorne came to an end. A six-day sale of the effects was conducted on the premises by Messrs. Furber, Price and Furber, between April 8th and 15th of that year.

The catalogues make fascinating reading. The House, which came first, contained little of value in furnishings or decorations (one looks in vain for some vestiges of Lord Cremorne's collection of pictures); but, the well-documented sanitary arrangements have some historical interest: '226 The well-made range of polished pine Washstands with vein marble top and back, fitted with 6 Jennings patent lift-up basins, [and] 6 brass taps'; '227. The three-division slate Urinal by Jennings, with iron gratings'. '228. A Ditto'. '229. The two water closets, Jennings's patent, with mahogany seats and risers.'

The last day, April 15th, saw the dispersal of The Decorations, Gas Illuminations, Statues, Fountains, Grand Bay Trees, Greenhouse Plants, and Outdoor Effects. Some of the well-known eye-catchers in the Gardens are listed: '1363. A Sylvester's Fairy Fountain, the peculiar construction of which renders it available for any Stage or Garden, from its beautiful and varied effects, with hose, machinery, &c.'; '1376. The Circular Dancing Platform in 32 Section measuring about 360 feet in circumference'; '1377. The ornamental iron Panel Enclosure to the same, 16 pairs of iron pillars with ornamental arches and gas jets…'; '1378. The complete erection of the Pagoda-shaped Orchestra, fitted with an 8-light gasolier, 16 2-light bracket ditto, with zinc roof, dressing room and 7 cabinets [supper-boxes] under…'; and '1393 The stalactite Rustic Erection of the "Gipsy Cave" with interior scenery and fittings'.

The site quickly followed the fate of most of London's Pleasure Gardens, falling a victim to housing and industrial development. Simpson's widow let the land out in building plots which were speedily covered. But even in Wroth's day (1907) something of the old 'pleasannce' remained: 'a grotto or bower surmounted by some of the plaster goddesses of Cremorne'; and the famous 'iron entrance-gates' which were removed to the 'premises of the Royal Chelsea Brewery'. Since then much of the late nineteenth century layout has also disappeared. Lots Road Power Station occupies what must have been Cremorne's river-frontage; while, at the time of writing, red-fronted sky-scraper flats are going up on what would have once been its extensive lawns. And now only some of the road-names – Stadium, Ashburnham and Cremorne itself – and the gates, which (it is understood) have happily been preserved by the Chelsea Borough Council and are to be re-erected in some appropriate place, will be there to recall the former existence of the last of London's great Pleasure Gardens.

1947

BIBLIOGRAPHY

British Museum (National Library). Folio Volume, labelled *Cremorne Gardens Entertainments* (1880 c.g.), containing bills, news-cuttings, and views, &c., covering the period of the Gardens' history, 1831-77;. Warwick Wroth, *Cremorne and the later London Gardens*, 1907 (with earlier Bibl.).

An Attempt to Grow Raw Silk in Chelsea in the Eighteenth Century

Barbara Smith

In the comparatively peaceful days of 1718, the future must have looked promising, even exciting, to Mr. John Apletree. The war with Spain was over and many domestic schemes to make money were springing up, stimulated, in part, by the prospect of a period of stability. The government actively encouraged new processes, especially schemes which would provide employment for the poor. On 23rd May, 1718, Mr. Apletree took out a Royal patent to cover his "way of raising Silk in this our Kingdom of Great Britain to as great a perfection as in any part of Europe, " and during the next few months he established a company to grow silk in Chelsea called the Raw Silk Undertaking or sometimes the Raw Silk Company.

That John Apletree of Worcester should embark on a scheme to raise silkworms for raw silk in Chelsea is not at all surprising. In the early 18th century, the introduction of new, and preferably, exotic plants and fruits was part of the general curiosity and willingness to experiment. Fascination with the mulberry tree was not new, however. The tree had been introduced into England during the reign of Henry VIII. The earliest one on record was planted at Syon House in 1548 and is still flourishing today.

By the reign of James I, the English wished to break the French monopoly in silk. As silkworms were fed on mulberry leaves, James I wrote numerous letters to various landowners, encouraging them to plant mulberry trees and various unsuccessful attempts were made to raise raw silk in England. By the 18th century, the expansion of the thriving silk industry was hampered by having to import expensive raw material. Thus the Raw Silk Undertaking was conceived.

If raw silk was a promising product, Chelsea was also a promising and agreeable site for a mulberry plantation. The Physick Gardens had been established in 1613 with Sir Hans Sloane's generous patronage. Sir Robert Walpole had formed his own large collection of exotics in his garden adjacent to the Royal Hospital grounds. In the neighbourhood of King's Road, were several nursery gardens which "besides furnishing the choicest variety of early-raised flowers, have each succeeding season something new to present to the botanical world".

In 1718, the development of the Raw Silk company was supported and encouraged by Mr. Henry Barham; a writer on natural history. He wrote pamphlets commending Chelsea Park, a pleasant open field, as a suitable site for a mulberry plantation. He took a house in Church Lane (now Old Church Street) which was one of the boundaries of the Park and even paid the rates on behalf of the company for the years 1718, 1719 and possibly 1720.

Chelsea in 1718/19 was still a small quiet village and a peaceful retreat. Chelsea Park was formerly part of the grounds of Sir Thomas More's estate and comprised 40 acres of land bounded by the modern streets of Fulham Road and King's Road, Park Walk and Old Church Street. Almost 2,000 mulberry trees were planted by the Company, and houses to keep the silkworms and their eggs protected were built.

The essential requirements were warmth and food. John Apletree's patent promised that his invention, an evaporating stove, would keep the eggs of the silkworm at a uniform temperature and that he "hath a certain and infallible method of feeding the said worms with undoubted success be it ever so wett". Henry Barham was more ambitious and claimed... "tis evident that the profit of this undertaking will make an increase beyond all the trades now to be undertaken in the knowledge of man in the World."

In great contrast to the quiet mulberry orchard in Chelsea village was the other centre of the Company's activities - the area in the City known as Exchange Alley. By the end of 1718 and 1719, when the Company became organised, Exchange Alley was feverish with excitement. Joint stock companies such as the Raw Silk Company were being established at an enormous rate and fortunes were being made as speculative capital poured into the city. The Royal Patent granted to Apletree was enrolled in Chancery and proposals for the organisation of the company were published.

The next most important step was the selling of shares in Exchange Alley. Defoe wrote in his Anatomy of Exchange Alley, "stock-jobbing is play: a Box and dice may be less dangerous!" Carswell wrote, "the crowd in Exchange Alley was as thick and almost as aristocratic as it was at St. James." The heady success of the South Seas Company and others, and the almost unbelievable fortunes being made, must have created a most exciting atmosphere.

The subscription for the Raw Silk Undertaking was opened in January 29th, 1720, at the Marine Coffee Shop, Exchange Alley, with an authorized capital of £1,000,000. The Raw Silk Company was born at the centre of a whirlwind,

Meanwhile, in Chelsea, the Undertaking appeared to flourish. A lease of the Park for sixty years was granted by William Sloane (nephew of Sir Hans Sloane) to John Apletree and the Company began to pay rates in its own name in 1721. Two thousand mulberries of both the black and white variety were planted.

By 1721 it seems to have been both agreeable and fashionable to pay a visit to the mulberry plantation in Chelsea. The Weekly Journal of Saturday, 12th August, 1721, comments:

"We hear there is a great concourse of foreigners and others daily in Chelsea Park to see the Raw Silk Undertaking." Unfortunately, there seems to be no record of how the sale of the shares progressed but nine of the original share certificates issued to the Arundel family have survived.

In 1723, Ralph Thorsby, described in the *Dictionary of National Biography* as a painstaking diarist, records a visit to Chelsea in his diary. "I dined at Mr. Gales... I saw a sample there of the satin lately made at Chelsea of English silkworms for the Princess of Wales, which was very rich and beautiful."

Suddenly, in 1724, the world of mulberry trees and gently heated silkworms fell apart. The *London Gazette* of 24th April, 1724, carried this sad little advertisement:

"The creditors of John Apletree, late of Woodstock, Mercer, who have not received satisfaction for their debts, are desired to send an account of such their debts forthwith to Mr. Brace in Milk Street in order for their receiving satisfaction for the same."

The reasons for the failure of such a promising venture (successful at Lullingstone Castle in Kent during the 20th century) lies in the realm of speculation. Unfortunately, it seems that no company records remain to explain the collapse of the Raw Silk Undertaking. Possibly a clue lies in the statement by Henry Barham in 1719 when he reported that 2, 000 trees of both black and white mulberry were planted in Chelsea Park. Unfortunately, black mulberry leaves are too tough for the silkworms to feed on and this might have reduced their supply of food decisively.

Another possibility was the government's changing attitude to home industries, particularly textiles. Walpole began to implement a free trade policy in this period and import tax on raw silk was removed altogether in 1721, This move by the government must have been a severe blow to commercial confidence in the Raw Silk Undertaking and confidence was a valuable asset in the days following the collapse of the South Sea Bubble in 1720. T. S. Ashton describes the periods as a "mania of speculation: a crisis and finally universal stagnation." The trade in luxury commodities such as silk dried up.

In May 1724, a month after John Apletree became bankrupt, William Sloane apparently accepted the surrender of the Company's lease and granted a new lease of Chelsea Park to Sir Richard Manningham. In July, the new owner paid the rates on the 40 acres and three years later Chelsea Park was divided up into lots and sold off.

The only surviving trace in Chelsea of the Raw Silk Company is a black mulberry tree still flourishing in Elm Park Road and the names of Mulberry Walk and Appletree House in the Vale.

1971

THE CHELSEA PHYSIC GARDEN

Alan Paterson, N.H.D., M.Ed.,F.L.S. (ex-curator)

The first botanic gardens in Western Europe, and as we know them, in the world, were set up in the rich High Renaissance city-states of Northern Italy. Pisa had the first, in 1543. Two years later gardens in Padua and Florence were opened and the predominant university schools of medicine followed at Bologna, Leiden, Montpellier, Oxford and Edinburgh, in little over a century. Their titles varied: Hortus medicus, Hortus botanicus, Giardina dei Simplici, Jardin des Plantes or, in this country, Physic Garden. But their roles were similar, which were to grow plants for recognition and study for medicinal and general scientific use.

The Chelsea Physic Garden is unusual and perhaps unique amongst the numerous and varied institutions in Britain devoted to the scientific study of plants. Most botanists know it as the second oldest physic garden in England, about fifty years younger than the one at Oxford and nearly a hundred years older than the Royal Botanic Gardens at Kew.

The name needs at first to be clarified, since, amongst the early botanic gardens, Chelsea only has retained its original epithet. This gives rise to a confusion about its aims which is heightened by the knowledge that the garden was founded by and for the Worshipful Society of Apothecaries of London. Moreover, that was in 1673 when the word physic still had its original meaning of 'pertaining to things natural' as distinct from the metaphysical. The modern use of the word seems to refer only to the physic of doctors and hence visitors are apt to expect a garden devoted solely to the culture of medicinal herbs.

Here then, only two and a half miles from Piccadilly Circus lies, like an oasis, rather under four acres of some of the most intensively cultivated ground in the country. Since the Garden's inception the roles have been twofold: educational and scientific. These hold good today and a continuum of botany, medicine and related subjects can be traced through good times and bad for over 300 years.

Of course, the particular interest of apothecaries was with officinal plants. But in a period when Paracelcian ideas were still alive – that

Philip Miller

every plant would cure something, if only antidote and disorder could be brought together, every plant species was a potential remedy. Hence plants grown extended beyond those known (or currently believed) to be efficacious and were continually being added to by new species from new worlds.

It was not, however, at the beginning, in 1673, all plain sailing and clearly not all the early Gardeners (as the Curators were then termed) were up to the job of promoting a new botanic garden. Nevertheless within ten years from its foundation, and now in the care of John Watts, himself an Apothecary, its importance was sufficient for Paul Hermann, the Professor of Botany of Leiden University, to visit it. Watts returned his visit in 1683 to exchange seeds and plants with Leiden. So began a mutual exchange with other botanic gardens throughout the world, a process which has continued ever since (in 1975 for example, over 2, 500 packets of seeds were sent out and 1, 500 species received). Amongst the plants brought back by Watts from Leiden were four young Cedrus libani.

These were among the first to be planted in England and surprised the contemporary world by succeeding so well. The Chelsea cedars dominate all post seventeenth-century illustrations of the Garden: they took up so much space in the garden that two were felled in 1771. (The last, weakened by London's increasing atmospheric pollution, survived until 1904.)

John Evelyn, diarist and author of the famous *Sylva* came to Chelsea in 1685 and writes of plants he saw. He was particularly impressed by the 'subterraneous heat conveyed by a stove' which heated the conservatory. Unfortunately, in the 1690's, Watts appears to have lost interest and with his enthusiasm the Garden declined as well. Incomplete records of the next thirty years tell a confused story of monetary troubles and lack of direction. But help was at hand.

Having bought the Manor of Chelsea from Charles Cheyne in 1712, Dr. Hans Sloane had become owner of the Garden's freehold. By fortunate chance, Sloane, now a wealthy and influential man (he was created a baronet in 1716), had studied at the Garden. Now the Apothecaries appealed to him and in 1722 he virtually re-founded the Garden by granting a lease to the Society at £5 a year in perpetuity, laying out in legal terms conditions to guarantee the Garden's existence, "on condition that it be for ever kept up and maintained by the Company as a physick garden". To make sure that it was so kept, Sloane's Conveyance required fifty plant specimens from the Garden to be delivered annually to the Royal Society, until 2,000 pressed and mounted species had been received. In fact by 1795, when the flow ceased, the total reached 3,700.

Cheyne and Sloane are names well commemorated in this area, but the latter's memorials more truly lie in the Garden and with the British Museum which was founded with his collections and which included the herbarium sheets of the Garden's plants, now housed at the British Museum (Natural History) in South Kensington. They provide a valuable source of information about plants in cultivation during the eighteenth century.

Sloane's commensurate benefit to Chelsea was instigating the appointment of Philip Miller as Gardener in 1722. Miller became the greatest botanical horticulturist of his century, developing Chelsea as the finest Botanic Garden in the world; superlatives seem to become the order of the day when this man is discussed.

Miller's reign at Chelsea extended for nearly fifty years, during which time his famed *Dictionary of Gardening* ("Non erit Lexicon Hortulanorum, sed etiam Botanicorum" Linnaeus is reputed to have said of it), ran through eight editions during his lifetime. Carl von Linné, the great Swedish botanist, had paid a visit here in 1733 recording in his diary that "Miller of Chelsea permitted me to collect many plants in the garden." He was, however somewhat scornful of Miller's cautious approach to botanical innovation. Conservative by nature, Miller was slow to change his normal practice but in the seventh edition of his Dictionary he adopted Linnaeus' botanical classification and in the eighth the binomial nomenclature which Linnaeus had introduced nearly twenty years before. These innovations make it the first modern encyclopaedia of horticulture and it is still of value today.

For the time, Chelsea's facilities were good: in 1732, Sloane laid the foundation stone of a fine new greenhouse designed in the classical orangery mode and it was in use the following year. There were library and meeting rooms above and the main block was flanked by lean-to houses which were heated both by stoves and by beds of fermenting tan-bark. Sadly, his elegant structure was demolished in the middle of the nineteenth century when sewer construction undermined the foundations. This is the building shown on all the eighteenth and early nineteenth century prints of the garden.

Rysbrach's white marble statue of Sir Hans commissioned at this time by the Apothecaries, was originally erected here but moved to the present dominating position a few years later.

Miller was succeeded at Chelsea in 1770 by William Forsyth (after whom *Forsythia* is named). As Demonstrator of Plants, in 1773, Forsyth was joined by William Curtis, who was author of the *Flora Londinensis* "one of the most beautiful and accurate works on British plants" and originator of the *Botanical Magazine* which is still published and bears his name to this day.

In the next few decades, the Garden continued to flourish, though some of its activities had to be curtailed during the Napoleonic Wars (though these merely accentuated rather than caused the difficulties of obtaining new plants from abroad: Miller's correspondence, years before, is peppered with references to lost and delayed shipments and arrival of dead specimens. It is easy to forget now the problems of transport then experienced).

Subsequently a nineteenth century associate of the Garden, Nathaniel Bagshawe Ward, was of great importance in this context of transferring plant species across the world. The invention of 'Wardian Cases', like small, sealed, mobile greenhouses made possible the introduction of countless tropical plants to Europe and notably the transference of rubber (*Hevea brasiliensis*) to Ceylon and then Malaya from its South American home.

As the nineteenth century waxed, so the importance of the Garden waned, despite the extremely successful and well-attended lectures delivered by Professor John Lindley over 17 years from his appointment as Lecturer in Botany in 1836.

During the latter half of the century the Garden fell on hard times. There came another of the recurring financial crises. The Society of Apothecaries retrenched, dispensed with Lindley and his lectures, sacked its labourers, sold one glass-house and discontinued heating another, and appealed for money; by such drastic measures they just managed to keep the Garden going. The Physic Garden was, however, but one of their concerns. The Society played an important part in medical education, most of its members exchanging the old title of apothecary for that of general practitioner of medicine, while others became trading pharmacists, and during the century the importance of medical botany in their training grew less and less.

The Garden was certainly a financial strain, and the Society alleged that it was no longer suitable for the purposes of a botanic garden, because of the deleterious effects of increasing atmospheric pollution in London and the impoverished state of the soil, whose water table had been greatly lowered by the building of the Chelsea Embankment in 1874 which cut the Garden off from the river.

However, final closure was averted. As on earlier occasions, a few men of enterprise and vision realised its potentialities, notably the Director of the Royal Botanic Gardens, Kew, and the Professor of Botany at the Imperial College of Science; they urged upon the Treasury its continuing importance for botanical study. These men had been alerted by what can only be described as a local residents'

pressure group who feared, with good reason, that this historic garden would disappear under bricks and mortar as had so much of old Chelsea. (The beautiful Paradise Row opposite was razed at about this time.) The group can clearly be seen as a precursor of our own Society which has to be just as vigilant today, as we all know.

Their combined efforts in 1898 to save the Garden for posterity succeeded.

Accordingly, in 1899 the Chelsea Physic Garden passed into the administration of the London Parochial Charities. They appointed a Committee of Management, with representatives from the Royal Society, the Royal College of Physicians, the Society of Apothecaries and London University and other bodies and a new Curator, William Hales, to whom, with Professor Farmer of Imperial College, much of the present layout is due.

Designated a charity, the object of the Garden was stated as being concerned with education, scientific research and technical pharmacology. Hence its original interests were continued and embodied in a scheme which reflected the roles of many botanic gardens at the beginning of this century.

Links with education in the succeeding 75 years are obvious; the continual availability of the Garden to students of all ages and in the copious flow of the teaching specimens through schools and col-

The Physic Garden in the late eighteenth century

leges in London and beyond, are noteworthy. Those with research are implicit in the papers produced from work done on the Garden perhaps the most important being that on photoperiodism and vernalisation in plants by Professor Gregory in the '30's and '40's. In fulfilling the third role the Garden (while emphasising again the fact that it is not a herb garden *per se*) cultivates a wide range of officinal plants and maintains links with teaching hospitals and departments of pharmacognosy.

In the past, visitors entered the Garden by the old Students' Gate in Swan Walk. Though no longer used for entry this is still a viewing point for many people. Here a glimpse is obtained of a wide, formal, gravelled walk, the vista closed by a figure on a high plinth, the whole arched with trees. The profusion of plant growth in summer, far from overflowing the Garden seems to extend its bounds and also clothes the basically seventeenth century rectilinear plan. On each side paths branch off at right angles, that to the left down towards the river (now sadly cut off by the traffic-ridden Chelsea Embankment) while that to the right passes the culinary and officinal plants en route to the glass-house range.

Present-day students now come in by the West Gate in Royal Hospital Road but still find it useful to orientate themselves upon Rysbrack's statue of Sir Hans Sloane from where the cruciform ground-plan is apparent. From this point the main walk slopes down to the Embankment Gates. On either side, comprising therefore nearly a third of the whole area, are botanical order beds. It might be thought that this is a visually arid method of displaying plants, but it can clearly be seen not to be so. Nonetheless, aesthetic considerations, though not neglected (staff still use the eighteenth-century phrase "dressing the beds" when planting is being done) cannot be a prime concern. Here are around a hundred plant families proceeding like a great flora spread out page by page on the ground from (north to south, east to west) *Ranunculaceae* to *Saxifragaceae*, *Onagraceae* to *Labiatae* and *Plantaginaceae* to *Gramineae*. Except where a family possesses only woody members, the representative plants are mainly herbaceous.

To a keen plantsman these order beds are of perennial interest: to observe so graphically the relationships, diversity of form, structure and range within a plant family adds considerably to one's conceptual understanding of that group. They also show many fine species which, although eminently garden-worthy, are not generally available.

Any Botanic Garden must demonstrate plants from a wide range of habitats, and so below the eastern dicotyledon families is a long

Palm tree in flower in the Physic Garden

rock bed, a moist border and a pool. Many good plants can be found here in the pool, butomus (the flowering rush, a lovely British native) and *Pontederia cordata* flourish.

Around a huge Quercus ilex nearby is a small ericaceous collection of heathers, dwarf rhododendrons and associated plants. Summer drought is a problem and Himalayan primulas have perforce been planted in polythene lined beds.

Returning back up the Garden along the old wall by Swan Walk, visitors, at whatever time of the year they come, get an idea of this part of London's extraordinary mild microclimate, by the plants which succeed here. *Correa backhousiana* and *Dodonaea viscosa purpurea* flourish: there is a fine old *Styrax officinalis* and opposite, the loveliest tree in the whole garden, a magnificent *Koelreuteria paniculata*. This is perhaps the best specimen of the 'willow pattern tree' in this country.

Towards the glasshouses is a remarkable 30ft. high olive tree; no doubt the biggest in Britain. After last year's remarkable summer 71 lbs. of ripe olives were picked on 3rd December: this London crop (which we are currently eating) must be unique in the annals of English horticulture. In this north-east corner of the garden the culinary, current medicinal, and historical officinal herbs have recently been rearranged into beds which, it is hoped, will facilitate their study. To design a satisfactory herb garden is not easy if as wide a range of species as possible is required, as it is here. But a huge clipped bay offers a focal point from which the divisions, paved and grassed, can proceed. Certain plants appear in more than one category, especially as other groups are included: dye plants and species used in perfumery.

Along the north boundary run the glasshouses, Curator's house, and laboratory. These date mainly from 1900. The glasshouses again hold as representative a collection of species as possible for demonstration and teaching and offer controlled environments for research. In parallel with the wide availability of plant species for demonstration and study the research aspect of the garden continues. Several colleges of the University of London, Hospitals, the Botany Department of the British Museum (Natural History) have programmes of work in train. These include enquiry into production of D.N.A., cytological investigation of ferns (particularly Dryopteris), work on Mediterranean composites, especially Anacyclus, *Potamogeton spp* (pondweeds) and so on. Further research programmes are currently being planned.

Another important aspect is the growing of various cereals, rye, barley and wheat, to be injected with the fungus *Claviceps purpurea*. This is ergot, once greatly feared as a poisonous adulterant in flour, now a source of a valued drug: here new strains are being cultivated.

In the international botanical field, the Garden's Seed List goes out to some 300 other gardens; thus the exchange of species, as begun with Leiden almost 300 years ago, continues to flourish. Closer home, teaching specimens are supplied to schools and colleges and series of lectures are held here. Thus those reasons for which the Garden was founded, are still valid and still in use. And hence the 1899 scheme is still thought viable. Even in these vastly changed and changing times the availability of some 5,000 species of plants for study in Central London is truly remarkable.

1991

INDEX

One of the great pleasures of editing this book has been the opportunity of talking to so many of those who have contributed articles to *The Chelsea Report* over the years. I would like to thank them as well as those others whose enthusiasm and love of Chelsea has contributed so much to the creation of this publication.

The red anchor which appears on the title page is the logo of The Chelsea Society. It is derived from the ceramic mark of Chelsea China and dates from the mid-eighteenth century.

Every reasonable effort has been made to contact holders of copyright material which appears here. Holders of copyright material who have not been contacted are requested to write to the publishers.

Jane Dorrell

CREDITS

Cover illustration, Hugh Krall; pages 6, 13, 14, 55 & 57 (right), courtesy of The Royal Borough of Kensington and Chelsea; page 11, insert to *The Chelsea Society Report*, 1945; pages 15 & 18, courtesy of Christie's Images; pages 16 & 19, courtesy of the British Library; pages 25, 52, 66 and 78, Dennis Flanders; page 30 & 31, courtesy of the Trustees of the Sir John Soane's Museum; page 32, *The Chelsea Society Report*, 1995; page 36, Walter Burgess; page 38, age 17, by R. Bouyer, at age 36, by Joseph Severn, age 66 by F.W. Williams and J. Armytage; pages 40, 67, 73 & 80, photographs by Jane Dorrell; page 57 (left), The Chelsea Society; page 60, Norma Bull; page 64, *The Chelsea Society Report*, 1944-45; page 68, *The Chelsea Society Report*, 1998; page 69, photograph by Tom Pocock; page 74, *The Chelsea Society Report*, 1985, courtesy of Barry Fantoni; page 76, David Le Lay; pages 86, 89, 90, 99 & 103, private collections; page 92, Blickling Hall, The Lothian Collection, (National Trust), NTPL/John Hammond; page 93, The National Gallery of Cuba/Andrew Cravette; page 94, permission of Chelsea and Westminster Hospital, Arts and Health project; page 96, David Le Lay; page 102, *The Chelsea Society Report*, 1991; page 106, *The Chelsea Society Report*, 1947; pages 111, 113 & 114, courtesy of The Curator of the Chelsea Physic Garden; drawings on pages 55 & 57 by Clifford Hall.

First published in Great Britain by

Elliott & Thompson Ltd
27 John Street
London WC1N 2BX

Text © The Chelsea Society 2004

ISBN 1 904027 29 6

First edition

Book Design by Brad Thompson
Printed and bound in England by Cambridge Printing